
❖

DAVID
A Heart for God

DAVID
A Heart for God

Stuart Briscoe

While this book is designed for your personal enjoyment,
it is also intended for group study.
A Leader's Guide with Multiuse Transparency Masters
is available from your local bookstore
or from the publisher.

VICTOR BOOKS®
A DIVISION OF SCRIPTURE PRESS PUBLICATIONS INC.
USA CANADA ENGLAND

Second printing, 1988

Unless otherwise indicated, all Scripture quotations are from the *New King James Bible*, © 1979, 1980, 1982, Thomas Nelson, Inc., Publishers. Other references are from the *King James Version* (KJV).

Recommended Dewey Decimal Classification: 248.4
Suggested Subject Heading: CHRISTIAN LIVING

Library of Congress Catalog Card Number: 87-62490
ISBN: 0-89693-466-7

Contents

DAVID
A Heart for God

CHAPTER ONE

A Survey of Our Hearts

But the LORD said to Samuel, "Do not look at his appearance or at the height of his stature, because I have refused him. For the LORD does not see as man sees; for man looks at the outward appearance, but the LORD looks at the heart"

(1 Sam. 16:7).

Some people say we are a narcissistic generation. The word *narcissistic* is derived, of course, from the Greek mythological figure Narcissus, who became so obsessed with the reflection of himself that he saw in a mountain pool that he could think of nothing else. To be narcissistic then is to be absorbed with one's self. Indeed, some feel that this attitude is so widespread in today's Western society that they have given it the collective description, the "me generation."

This preoccupation with self—being exclusively attached to "me"—is one of the great problems in our society at the present hour. To be absorbed with self and, at the same time, to exist as a part of a society is to live in a mutually contradictory situation. A society can never survive if it is simply a collection of intrinsically self-oriented people.

If a society is to function and be productive, it will be because those who are intrinsically selfish begin to discover that another heart-attitude is necessary. A change of direction from self to servitude, from inward to outward, is needed. And if this need for change is true for society at large, it is doubly true for the church of Jesus Christ. I'm afraid the same spirit that pervades our society has spread to the people of God.

Preoccupation with self-esteem, or self-love, which the church has consistently resisted as a vice, has now all of a sudden become a virtue. It is coupled with an individualism in which we say the Lord is speaking to *me*, rarely to *us*. It is *my* ministry, *my* gifts, *my* vision.

Beloved, we have jumped the track.

Christians must concern themselves again in our time with a basic commitment to develop a heart for God. And I use the word *develop* advisedly. To develop a godly servant heart is necessary because servant attitudes don't come naturally to fallen human beings. We have to learn how to have a heart for God. We don't have to learn how to be selfish; that seems to be a natural instinct. Looking out for number one is something that is, because of sin, built into us.

King David, the monarch of ancient Israel, was one who learned to develop a heart for God. He became God's servant. He served God's purpose in his own generation, and it was a generation not at all unlike our own.

Be encouraged. David was a realist. He learned to expect no more than what God had promised. But he did not dare to settle for anything less.

Thus, to retune our hearts to be attentive to the will of God, and to reignite a genuine love for Him instead of continuing to develop an enamorment with ourselves, we will take a detailed, in-depth look into the life of David.

What was it that made this man—who easily had as many personal struggles as any of us—turn from himself to pursue a heart for God? Were there discernible steppingstones to his victories? How did he succeed in overcoming his own sins and weaknesses to the extent that he not only glorified the Lord, but also effected a change in the people of his own generation?

THE MAN AFTER GOD'S HEART

Israel wanted to be like all the other nations. She wanted a monarchy, the rule of a king. God had warned her against it, but she was adamant. In the end, God said yes, and Israel coronated Saul as her first king.

Saul was at first a humble man—so humble in fact that when he heard he was going to be appointed to reign over Israel, he literally went out and hid behind a pile of refuse. His family had to go out and get him.

But something changed. Early into his reign, it was obvious there were problems; many serious flaws marked his character. He would need to be replaced. But thirty-two years elapsed before it happened—thirty-two years of opportunity for Saul to repent and come to the point of being what God wanted him to be. He never did. In the end God spoke to him through the prophet Samuel and told him his kingdom was going to be given to another.

The Book of Samuel tells us what happened: "Then Samuel took the horn of oil and anointed him in the midst of his brothers; and the Spirit of the LORD came upon David from that day forward" (1 Sam. 16:13).

At first Samuel had looked at Eliab, the eldest son of Jesse, to be king. He was, after all, the oldest and the biggest. He looked the part. "But the LORD said to Samuel, 'Do not look at his appearance or at the height of his stature, because I have refused him. For the LORD does not see as man sees; for man looks at the outward appearance, but the LORD looks at the heart' " (1 Sam. 16:7). David would be God's choice.

At the very beginning of David's experiences as the king of Israel, we see a powerful statement concerning the human heart. Samuel, finding the man of God's choosing, is told to look not on the outside as man does, but to recognize that God looks on the heart.

THE HUMAN HEART

How often the human heart figures into what God has to say!

In 1 Samuel 12:20, Samuel said, "Do not fear. You have done all this wickedness; yet do not turn aside from following the LORD, but serve the LORD with all your heart." In

Scripture you will find that the heart symbolizes the part of us that is *designed to discern the truth*. Serving the Lord with all our hearts means, first of all, that the part of us designed to discern the truth must learn to discern the truth concerning the Lord. Our hearts must be prepared to be open to discover all that God has revealed of Himself.

The heart, that innermost part of our being, is designed by God to be thoroughly involved in all that He has in mind for us. But it can also lead us in the opposite direction.

In today's thought and language, while there is a physical sense in which we view the heart in terms of ventricles, valves, and veins, we also use the word in significantly different ways. For example, somebody is "good at heart." We learn things "by heart." It is said we get into things "heart and soul." If someone is courageous, we say he has a "heart of steel." If we want someone to show us a little compassion, we say, "Aw, come on, have a heart." If we feel deeply attached to something, we might hum a few bars of "I Left My Heart In San Francisco."

If a friend is unnerved about something, we encourage him to set his heart at rest. If we have a tremendous desire to achieve a certain goal, we set our hearts on it. When we take something very seriously, we take it to heart. A lady who is very open and transparent wears her heart on her sleeve. And if people are thoroughly committed to a task, they get into it with all their hearts.

The case rests. It is obvious that our modern use of the word *heart* as a symbol to describe inner attitudes is closely aligned to the biblical use of the word. Beyond being a mere physical organ, then, the heart symbolizes the very center of our being, the spiritual epicenter of our life. God has specifically and uniquely designed that innermost part of us to discern, to desire, to decide, to dedicate. What He has in mind is that all these actions of the heart might be done rightly, in accordance with His will.

GOD DEALS WITH OUR HEARTS

If God has designed the heart as the action-central of our lives, how does He deal with our hearts? For the answer, we turn again to the writings of Samuel. We read in 1 Samuel 9:18-19,

> Then Saul drew near to Samuel in the gate, and said, "Please tell me, where is the seer's house?" And Samuel answered Saul and said, "I am the seer. Go up before me to the high place, for you shall eat with me today; and tomorrow I will let you go and will tell you all that is in your heart."

Notice: "I will tell you all that is in your heart."

We have already seen that God examines the heart. He reads it, as it were. Then, He makes an evaluation of what He finds.

This truth is amplified very powerfully by our Lord Jesus as recorded for us in Mark 7. There, Jesus was talking to the Pharisees, who were particularly concerned with externals but not at all with internals, with the heart attitude. Jesus wanted to remind them that their concern, their strange concern with all that goes into a person and its potential for defiling them, was totally misplaced. What goes in from outside doesn't defile us; it is what comes out from inside that is corrupting. The problem is the heart. For out of the heart come evil thoughts, sexual immorality, theft, murder, adultery, greed, malice, deceit, lewdness, envy, slander, arrogance, and folly (see Mark 7:21-23).

First, then, God *examines* our hearts. This is something I'm afraid we very often carefully avoid thinking about. Like the Pharisees, most of us are so wrapped up with externals, that the thought of God's examining what is really going on inside us is something for which we generally give no concern.

A second way in which God deals with our hearts is by *touching* them. According to 1 Samuel 10:26, earlier in his reign Saul gathered together valiant men "whose hearts God had touched." What a delightful expression! It means that God, having examined their hearts, found that they were receptive to Him.

Our hearts are touched when we say, "God, go ahead and do in my heart what needs to be done. Take what is wrong there and rectify it. Cleanse it. Straighten me out, Lord, touch my heart." A parallel to this in the New Testament is Ephesians 3 where we are reminded by Paul that Christ will dwell in our hearts by faith. In other words, God will so touch our hearts that He will do nothing less than send the crucified risen Christ by His Spirit into our hearts to put the imprimatur of God upon them.

Third, God *changes* our hearts. When God first had dealings with Saul, He changed his heart. At the outset, Saul began to go the way the Lord wanted him to go; he desired to serve the Lord. He had, at first, discerned the truth of God.

A great need for all of us is to continue to stay open to the work of God in our hearts. Saul started well, but he failed.

Christian, be warned. Guard your heart lest it grow immune to the work of God. Let Him know that you desperately want His touch upon your heart. Don't become weary of allowing Christ continually to bring to you that needed change of attitude, intent, ambition, or aspiration. Permit the changes to occur that come as Christ dwells in your heart and transforms you from within.

When we discuss the matter of the heart, then, we are referring to the inner part of ourselves that God has designed specifically and with which He deals very, very seriously indeed. Our major concern must be with what we allow Him to do there.

CHAPTER TWO

The Heart
of the King

And Samuel said to Saul, "You have done fool-
ishly. You have not kept the commandment of
the LORD your God, which He commanded you.
For now the LORD would have established your
kingdom over Israel forever. But now your
kingdom shall not continue. The LORD has
sought for Himself a man after His own heart,
and the LORD has commanded him to be com-
mander over His people, because you have not
kept what the LORD commanded you" (1 Sam.
13:13-14).

Why is David's life our model as we seek to develop a heart for God?

The Lord said certain things about the heart of this king, this servant, this man who was going to be so wonderfully used of Him. God's desire was for a man "after His own heart" (1 Sam. 13:14). We never have a description of what exactly that means, but we can arrive at it by arguing the negative, by contrasting David with Saul. Once we see that David was the man after God's own heart, we also understand that Saul was *not* the man after His own heart. And there are plenty of details available. In God's evaluation of Saul's heart, we are shown exactly what was wrong.

SAUL THE SUSPECT

The first thing we notice about Saul is that he was decidedly suspect in his *dependence* upon God. In 1 Samuel 13 Samuel had told Saul, "Now, listen, Saul. Go away to a certain place for seven days. Wait for me there. Don't do anything until I come. And when I come I will tell you exactly what the Lord wants you to do. Have you got that?"

"Yes."

"What have I told you to do?"

"I've got to wait seven days until you come and tell me what to do. I must not do anything until you come and tell me what God wants me to do."

"Right. Off you go, Saul."

Off he went. Seven days passed. Toward the end of the seventh day, there was still no Samuel. Saul became anxious. He decided the only thing to do was go right ahead, independently of God, and take matters into his own hands. Remember, the one thing he had been told to do was wait upon the Lord. But he did not want to wait. Never mind that the seven days were not quite up. He opted for independence from God.

It may seem to you a small matter in this particular instance. You probably could not make a case against Saul in today's judicial system. But what God discerned as He looked at the heart of Saul was a fundamental attitude that said Saul was going to do what he wanted to do. Saul was impetuous and independent, and had a heart for doing his own thing. That was how he had been, and that was how he was going to be.

God spoke to Saul through Samuel and said, "I've examined your heart, and I realize that you are very suspect in the area of dependence. As far as I'm concerned, unless there is a radical change in this area, you will not be the man after My own heart."

To test things out once and for all, God issued a final exam. In 1 Samuel 15, we read that God told Saul to destroy the Amalekites. It is a horrible story. Saul was to utterly destroy them, leaving absolutely no exceptions. He had to get rid of their livestock, their children, and all the adults. They were to be utterly liquidated.

What happened? Saul partially obeyed the Lord. He obeyed the part he agreed with and disobeyed the rest of the instructions. The frightening thing is that Saul was so much like you and me and the majority of our fellow Christians.

Secondly, Saul was suspect not only in his dependence, but also in his *obedience*. And I tell you, when we are suspect in both our dependence and our obedience, we have a problem as far as God is concerned. Basically, there are two things we are called to do: we are to depend on His strength and be obedient to His Word. If we can't handle being dependent and obedient, we have major heart trouble. Literally. And we will never become the kind of people who have a heart for God.

Another area where Saul's flaws showed up was in the exercise of his conscience. Watch how he stooped; he was ready to convey false impressions. After he had gone to the Amalekites and had done as he pleased, he went to Samuel and said, "Well, Hallelujah, Amen, Praise the Lord. We've had a great time. I've done everything the Lord told me to do. Glory!"

Samuel looked at him and said, "If you have done all that God told you to do, what is the lowing of the oxen I hear, and the bleating of the sheep? If you had done what God told you to do, there would be no noise from the oxen and the sheep."

Deep down in his heart, Saul knew precisely what was going on. He saw his area of disobedience. His conscience might have said, "Saul, back off on this thing. Don't pretend. God knows your heart. Samuel has a discerning spirit that is seeing right through you."

But Saul decided to pretend anyway. He fooled himself into conveying a false impression. His conscience had become seared, and it did not bother him a bit.

PASSING THE BUCK

Saul was not at all averse to communicating false information. When Samuel began to question him about why he didn't do what God told him, he said, "Well, it was the soldiers. It was their decision. They decided to keep some of the best sheep and cattle so we might offer them as a sacrifice to the Lord." Right, Saul. Disobey God for *religious* reasons!

It was not the soldiers' decision. Saul was in charge of those troops. It was his decision. Nor had they captured the animals to offer to the Lord. They had kept them for themselves. Visions of lamb chops and charbroiled steaks danced in their heads! Saul moved from a ploy to convey a false impression to communicating false information. The problem with Saul was no longer his being cagey; he was an out-and-out liar.

After he had been exposed, he still stuck to his story. With pious platitudes he said, "I *did* obey the Lord!"

Samuel shook his head no. "I'm sorry, Saul, you're through. This is not the kind of heart God is looking for. You aren't concerned about the things of God. You're not a man after God's own heart."

One more thing about Saul is disturbing. This fallen king, who once possessed almost every gift and endowment heaven had to offer, *repented.* He wept, he moaned, he pleaded. But this was one time in Israel's dealings with God when an act of remorse was not honored. God's verdict was, "It's over, Saul. Your pattern of self-will is irreversibly established." His sorrow was not that he sinned, but that he got caught. The reign of Saul was history.

DAVID THE MODEL

With Saul as the negative example, we can make some educated guesses concerning what the man after God's own heart was like. Let's look at some things about King David from the Psalms.

In Psalm 61:1-4 we read,

> Hear my cry, O God;
> Attend to my prayer
> From the end of the earth I will cry to You.
> When my heart is overwhelmed;
> Lead me to the rock that is higher than I.
> For You have been a shelter for me,
> And a strong tower from the enemy.

I will abide in Your tabernacle forever;
I will trust in the shelter of Your wings. Selah

Notice the difference here between Saul and David. When it came to dependence upon the Lord, Saul took matters into his own hands. But David prayed, "Lord, I cry to You. I pray to You. I call to You, because my heart is faint. I depend upon You because I need You desperately. You are like a rock to me. You are like a refuge to me. You are a strong tower for me. I take shelter constantly under Your wings." There is the man after God's own heart.

Let me ask, are you depending on the Lord in your marriage and its stresses, or do you contemplate turning to run? Pastor, will you stick with the ministry while others are bailing out in distrust and disobedience? Of course it's hard. Life is hard. But we are not called to ease and popular acclaim. We are told instead to pursue the spiritual life, to cultivate our hearts for God.

FINE-TUNING THE HEART

The next thing we notice about David is that he was busy working on an obedient heart. His beautiful expression of faith in Psalm 40:8 was, "I delight to do Your will, O my God,/And Your law is within my heart." Think about that for a minute. What was David's desire? Above all else he desired to learn what it meant to be obedient. He purposed to find new ways honestly and genuinely to discover God's will and do it.

Now remember, as we begin to explore David's life story, we will not find a perfect man. He was a flawed, struggling man who was as weak and sinful as Saul and the rest of us. The difference is that when it came to a dependent heart, Saul was independent. When it came to being obedient, Saul had an alternate agenda. Regarding honest, genuine integrity, Saul whitewashed his sins. He emerged consistently a big phony. But David? Although he shared many of Saul's same weaknesses, he chose instead to strive for obedience, and he developed a heart for God.

I love to preach in Anglican churches in Great Britain because, at the point in the liturgy when the minister steps into the pulpit, before he ever opens the Scriptures to preach the sermon, he repeats the prayer of David, "Let the words of my mouth and the meditation of my heart/Be acceptable in Your sight,/ O Lord, my strength and my redeemer" (Ps. 19:14). When David first wrote those words, he wanted to be finely tuned to the will of God, even in the meditations of his heart, in the words of his mouth, in the inner workings of his life. What a contrast with Saul, who sought to do only a minimal amount of God's bidding.

Psalm 139 finishes with these words: "Search me, O God, and know my heart;/Try me, and know my anxieties;/And see if there is any wicked way in me,/And lead me in the way everlasting." See the difference between the heart of Saul and the heart of David?

David wanted his heart to be openly transparent before God. He said, "Search my heart. Know my heart. Try me. Test me."

WHAT GOD IS AFTER

Do you know what God is looking for in our world today? Exactly what He was looking for in David's day—men and women after His own heart. That is why the Lord chose Jesse's number eight son. "Oh, he's out looking after the sheep," David's brothers had answered cynically when the Lord came searching for a king. They put him down every way they could. After all, he was a mere kid. But God saw his heart.

Incidentally, God is not against externals. He is all for beauty, but He is never misled by it. David, after all, was a handsome, clean-cut, ruddy-faced, suntanned, lively, virile young man. Those characteristics did not determine he was to be king, however. No, while human beings look on the outside, God looks on the heart.

One of the hardest lessons we have to learn in our day and age is that internals are more important than externals. The reason we need to be concerned about our heart attitudes is that we have gotten ourselves too wrapped up in image making and packaging, too involved in projecting what we want projected and marketing what we want marketed. There is a very real danger that we well might be the generation, more than any other, primarily concerned with external appearance at the expense of what really goes on in the heart.

Put in a very simple way—God is far more concerned about character than He is about reputation. Reputation is what we are able to project, or what people are able to perceive and what they think we are. Character is what God knows we are, what we are like when no one is watching. We can package, we can perform, we can project, we can promote, and we can pretend. What is scary is that when we are through, we have something in which God has no interest. The difference between character and reputation is something that ought to be constantly burning into our hearts and minds.

The heart that God is looking for is not perfect, because He knows He won't find one. What He is looking for is the heart of an honest, genuine, repentant person. Is that person you? If so, may I invite you to pray, "Lord, when I consider myself before You, and I know my heart before You, and I see how wrongly I discern and how badly I decide, my heart breaks before You. I humble myself before You and ask that my heart might be placed in Your mighty hand that You might touch it and change it."

CHAPTER THREE

The Hardened Heart

Then Samuel took the horn of oil and anointed him in the midst of his brothers; and the Spirit of the LORD came upon David from that day forward. So Samuel arose and went to Ramah.

But the Spirit of the LORD departed from Saul, and a distressing spirit from the LORD troubled him. And Saul's servants said to him, "Surely, a distressing spirit from God is troubling you. Let our master now command your servants, who are before you, to seek out a man who is a skillful player on the harp; and it shall be that he will play it with his hand when the distressing spirit from God is upon you, and you shall be well."

So Saul said to his servants, "Provide me now a man who can play well, and bring him to me." Then one of the servants answered and said, "Look, I have seen a son of Jesse the Bethlehemite, who is skillful in playing, a mighty man of valor, a man of war, prudent in speech, and a handsome person; and the LORD is with him."

Therefore Saul sent messengers to Jesse, and said, "Send me your son David, who is with the sheep." And Jesse took a donkey loaded with bread, a skin of wine, and a young goat, and sent them by his son David to Saul. So David came to Saul and stood before him. And he loved him greatly, and he became his armorbearer. Then Saul sent to Jesse, saying, "Please let David stand before me for he has found favor in my sight."

And so it was, whenever the spirit from God was upon Saul, that David would take a harp and play it with his hand. Then Saul would become refreshed and well, and the distressing spirit would depart from him (1 Sam. 16:13-23).

The decline of Saul was a terrible thing to see. The ascendancy of David, on the other hand, was a beautiful thing to behold.

It becomes rather obvious as we read the Scripture that the decline of the one and the ascendancy of the other were intimately linked with each one's experience of the Holy Spirit. The Scriptures teach that the Spirit of the Lord departed from Saul but came mightily upon David. It is the relationship of Saul with the Spirit of the Lord departing from him and the relationship of David to the Holy Spirit mightily upon him *daily* that is the key to the declension of one and the ascendancy of the other. Read again through the record in 1 Samuel 16:13-23 at the opening of this chapter.

While it is sometimes difficult to draw direct parallels between the experience of Old Testament saints and the experience of Christian people today, the message here is unequivocally clear: if we are in spiritual decline or apostacy, it is because of our lack of relationship with the Holy Spirit. And if we are in ascendancy or spiritual growth, it has to do with our intimacy and openness with the Spirit of God.

SAUL AND THE HOLY SPIRIT

It is important for us to recognize that Saul had a powerful experience of the Spirit of God.

According to 1 Samuel 10:10, the Spirit of the Lord came

upon him in power: "When they came there to the hill, there was a group of prophets to meet him; then the Spirit of God came upon him, and he prophesied among them." Clearly, the Holy Spirit came upon him. This event was a direct fulfillment of the promise of God, by the way, contained in 1 Samuel 10:6: "Then the Spirit of the LORD will come upon you, and you will prophesy with them and be turned into another man."

We may ask ourselves, "Why did Saul have this very dramatic experience?"

1. An evidence for Saul

First of all, it was to be evidence of God's choosing him for His particular ministry. The Spirit of the Lord coming upon him was evidence to Saul that this was really something *God* was doing.

Think about it for a moment. They had never had a king in Israel. The whole idea was brand new. And Saul, of all people!

Remember, when he was told he was going to be king, he hid behind the baggage and got himself out of sight. For him to accept the truth that he had been chosen by God to become the first king of Israel was a landmark struggle. He needed some degree of authentication in his own heart, a sense of assurance.

Saul was not the only one whose confidence was given a boost by the Holy Spirit. Saul's contemporaries were not going to accept readily the thought of his being king. They had known him since he was a young boy. Our Lord Himself said a prophet is not without honor except in his own country. The very idea that young Saul—this humble, frightened youngster, tall and handsome, but rather weak—was to be king of Israel would have been ludicrous to his contemporaries. The Spirit of the Lord came upon him so that they, too, might have clear evidence that God was at work in his life.

Notice the way this occurrence was made evident. Saul was told that various things would happen to him immediately after he had been anointed. Those things did occur, and the final incident took place as he went back to his hometown. A group of people came down from the hills—they were what I would call "Old Testament charismatics"—singing and dancing, playing their instruments and prophesying. They were engaging in ecstatic spiritual experiences. What happened? Saul joined them and began to sing and dance. His actions impressed his contemporaries because they said, "Has Saul joined the prophets too?" In all this, God established Saul with a sense of credibility among the people with whom he lived.

A similar event happened in the New Testament. On the day of Pentecost, as the Spirit of God came upon the one hundred twenty frightened believers, they became very bold. They had a great sense of assurance. But, beyond that, they were given a remarkable credibility with the people around them. Why? Because they spoke in languages that everyone around them understood. There was an ecstasy, an evidence of spiritual gift, because of the fact that the Holy Spirit had come upon them.

Christians differ in their understanding of the place of spiritual gifts in today's world, but there is no doubt that in Saul's day and in the early years of the church God saw fit to demonstrate the power of the Holy Spirit mightily upon the people by the gifts. He gave assurance to the people concerned and credibility among the heathen to whom they were sent to minister. And the first reason the Spirit came upon Saul was to provide evidence that he was God's choice for Israel's king.

2. The power for Saul to reign

Second, the Spirit came upon him for power. It was one thing to call Saul to be king. It was another thing to give him the equipment to reign. The equipment for being the king was the power of the Holy Spirit.

In 1 Samuel 11:6, God came upon Saul in power and motivated him in a way he had never been motivated before. "Then the Spirit of God came upon Saul when he heard this news, and his anger was greatly aroused." His anger here, by the way, was an anger against sin. He was able to accomplish things he never dreamed possible. And this, of course, is what the Holy Spirit does when He comes upon His people, individually or collectively: He gives them assurance, credibility, and discernment, and He empowers them for God's work. Without the Holy Spirit we are powerless to do anything in the spiritual realm. The psalmist said, "Unless the LORD builds the house,/They labor in vain who build it" (Ps. 127:1). That is as true in families as it is in kingdoms.

In other words, if we go into God's work without God's power, we are wasting our time. God has always promised His Spirit to His people. We can with confidence rely on the fact that the Holy Spirit dwells within us if we have come to Christ in repentance and faith. The indwelling Spirit will give us the power for service that we need, the courage to meet the situations we face, and the assurance that we are on the side of the angels. So it was with Saul. The Spirit of the Lord came upon him for God's empowering to rule as king of Israel.

3. Saul's life was changed

There was a third reason the Holy Spirit gripped Saul's life. As we read in 1 Samuel 10, when the Spirit of God came upon Saul, he was changed into a new man.

Let's face it. If the Holy Spirit is going to give us credibility among the people, then it is necessary to have power to do God's will and to have a change in our lives. Who is the agent of this change? The Spirit of the living God. The Holy Spirit came upon Saul as He comes upon Christian people today, to bring a change in their lives that brings them more and more into the image of God. That is what happened to King Saul.

It is a terrible shame, therefore, for us to discover that the Spirit of the Lord having come upon Saul (see 1 Sam. 10), so soon departed from him (see 1 Sam. 16). Why should such a thing happen? What does it mean? And most urgently, what is its significance for today—can this tragedy happen to us?

THE SPIRIT DEPARTS FROM SAUL

God had determined that Saul was totally unsuited for fulfilling His purpose. Although he was called to be the first king of Israel, to lead the people of Israel to become a nation after God's own heart, Saul could not lead them because he was not a man after God's own heart. Let me break the problem down into three areas.

1. Saul was unsuitable

A leader, any leader, must come to grips with the fact that he will not lead people beyond where he himself is. And if in the case of a Christian leader he is nowhere near where God wants him to be, he cannot therefore lead God's people. God will declare him unsuited for the task. He will become a person who may have the office but who lacks the godliness and the credibility required for the job. Unless he has the heart to repent, he will never fulfill God's purpose. God reserves the right to place that person on the shelf.

The apostle Paul had a concern in this area for his own ministry, if you can believe that. He explained it by using the analogy of an athlete training for the ancient games. We all know the discipline and dedication necessary for an athlete to achieve victory, to make the goal. The apostle said, "I am like an athlete when it comes to my ministry. I am determined to fulfill the role God has for me. So I buffet my body. I really train hard. I discipline totally. I apply myself exclusively to God's will. Because if I don't, I may be disqualified" (see 1 Cor. 9:24-27).

This message is serious and sobering. It applies not only to King Saul and the apostle Paul but also to every pastor, every deacon, and every elder. It is a warning to the Sunday school teacher, the youth club leader, the neighborhood group leader, the one teaching a small group— anyone professing to lead other people to Christian maturity.

God will not tolerate people who are called to lead but who do not continue in the power of the Spirit of God. We cannot disobey God, transgress His righteousness, and get away with it. If we do, we will be history. The Lord would sooner move us out of the way and give the job to somebody who will do it in the Spirit than to let us go on in error. This is a warning of the first order to those of us who may grow lax and careless in our areas of spiritual responsibility. Saul proved himself totally unsuitable to God's purpose, and the Holy Spirit left him.

2. Saul was unusable

Second, Saul proved himself to be utterly unusable in God's service. The kingly vision with which he began disappeared; he lost his cutting edge. The great start suddenly fizzled into utter disaster. All the trappings of royalty were still there. The sense of majesty did not change. But the man who was once God's man could no longer function as king over Israel. He was an ornate, empty shell, utterly unusable in God's service. God withdrew His authenticating and enabling Spirit, and though Saul went through the motions and said all the right things, he was finished as a spiritual leader.

I remember visiting the historic city of Ephesus years ago. I marveled at the memory of that great city. It was encouraging to recall the great church that Paul founded there. We walked down to the huge arena, the one in which the crowds had gathered to rebel against the Christians because they were turning the city inside out and upside down. We saw the area where Paul taught daily in the school of Tyrannus, training those persons he sent out to evangelize and establish churches in the crescent of cities around Ephesus. I thought of the wonderful Epistle to the Ephesians Paul had written. What a glorious church it was.

But today? Ephesus is an empty shell. I looked in the surrounding towns for a church, but I couldn't find a single one. We made inquiries as to whether there were any Christians in the area. Nobody knew of any.

Then I was reminded of the letters to the seven churches in Revelation, specifically the one the Lord Jesus sent to the church at Ephesus. Unless they returned to their first love, they were told, He would withdraw their candlestick. Unless they repented, their authority would be removed. He would not tolerate their laxity in loving God. And if you go to Ephesus today, you will witness the most glaring evidence of a removed candlestick you could ever hope to see.

Or you can look closer to home. Throughout the churches in America today, you will see the landscape littered with the remaining wreckage of people who once served God well. They are nowhere to be seen in the spiritual service of God. Oh, they may still be on the job. But the glory, the holiness, is gone. Shipwreck after shipwreck remains of people who have fallen on the shoals and the sharp, ragged-edged rocks of their own lack of discipline and perseverance. They were tempted by new truth, new ethics, and new lovers, and the Spirit of God departed from them. They are rusting hulks of what they were called to be, and they are an embarrassment to the church today.

3. Saul was immovable

The reason Saul was unusable in God's service was that

he was immovable in his heart. He would not give in and repent. You see, God examines the *heart*. He looks for people who are seeking after His own heart. The more God looked at Saul, the more He saw that though Saul had every opportunity through God's patience and mercy to repent and become His man again, he turned down every opportunity.

What were those opportunities? God provided David, the one who was to supersede him as king, to soothe Saul's troubled spirit with the psalms of Israel.

Whenever Saul was depressed, David was called to minister to him with his harp and psalms. Saul responded so positively to young David that David became his armorbearer. The king asked Jesse, David's father, to allow his youngest son to become part of the intimate royal household, to be close to him day after day, night after night.

THE FIRST THIRTY YEARS WAR

The grace and patience of God were unbelievable in the case of Saul. The king was told over thirty years before he left the throne that he would not continue to rule. Why did God allow thirty years to elapse? God was patiently giving him the opportunity to repent. He placed the man after His own heart in an intimate relationship with Saul. That is just like God in His grace, isn't it? But the tragedy is we often don't understand that the goodness of God is designed to lead us to repentance, not to be supportive of us in our sin.

Saul was a classic example. The patience of God gave him thirty years, which he wasted. The grace of God gave him a man after His own heart, whom he eventually tried to destroy. Nothing but repentance will ever change an arrogant, hard, self-centered, independent, disobedient heart. Saul would not repent, and the Spirit of the Lord departed from him.

But you say, "I thought he repented."

On the surface he repented. But there are different levels of repentance. True repentance is when we are heartbroken over sin. But there is also a kind of repentance that weeps bitter tears because we have been *caught*. It is a repentance that is *embarrassed* to death because the word is out about what we have done. That repentance is superficial.

Godly repentance works godly sorrow in our hearts. It is not sorrow only for the consequences of our sin, or for the fact that we got caught and everybody knows. Mature repentance means being sorry for the sin itself and turning away from it.

True repentance was utterly foreign to Saul. He was not ready for the change of heart that repentance requires.

YOU DON'T REMAIN ON "EMPTY"

The Spirit of the Lord departed from Saul. If that is difficult to accept, then hold onto your seat. Because the next thing that happened is even worse. "The spirit of the LORD departed from Saul, and an evil spirit from the LORD troubled him" (1 Sam. 16:14 KJV). If you read back through the whole passage, this concept of the evil spirit from the Lord troubling Saul is repeated. It is something that we may find extremely difficult to understand, but it is a reality with which we Christians must come to grips.

People look at the expression "evil spirit from the LORD," and they say, "An evil spirit is a demon. The Lord is sovereign over all things. If God wants to send a demon to disobedient people, it is possible for that person to become demon-possessed."

Others say the word translated "evil" here can also mean "bad" or "deteriorating." Therefore, what the writer was referring to was not demonic possession but a psychological breakdown, an emotional collapse. Still others would say, "Since God sent a specific evil spirit, it was far worse than demon-possession or psychological imbalance."

As we acknowledge these different possibilities, there are several things about which we can be completely sure. Number one, after the Spirit of the Lord departed from Saul, he had all kinds of what we today would term psychological illnesses. If a modern psychologist could put Saul on the couch, he or she could find melancholia, excruciating paranoia, bizzare emotional instability, and homicidal tendencies. When it came to irrational behavior, Saul had become king in that department. In other words, he had fallen apart.

Second, we know that later in his life he started dabbling in the occult. Whether he did earlier in life, we are not told. Let me say it plainly: those who begin to toy with the occult—at whatever level—are playing with black fire. They are laying themselves open to all kinds of satanic activity. If you are involved in any of it—horoscopes, palm reading, Tarot cards—*stop it!* There is no question that later in his life Saul showed signs of satanic oppression. But even then, the Lord was involved in what happened to him.

Are we saying the Lord allows satanic activity? Has the Lord ordained that spiritual misbehavior will have psychological ramifications? To both these questions, the answer is yes. Christians will disagree on the details—and I would have to say in all honesty that I have never met anybody that I would categorically say is demon-possessed—but I am not saying it doesn't happen, because I believe my New Testament. People who work in primitive areas of the world, where people worship Satan himself and live in the pit of hell, report that demons are deeply active there. I also believe that the more our society turns away from the Word of God, the church of God, and the Spirit of God, the more the possibility of demonic activity has to be taken into consideration.

And, we can say this: the Lord was certainly involved even in Saul's turning away. He has ordained that spiritual misbehavior will have all kinds of psychological ramifications. Why do some people go into deep, deep depression? Sometimes, not always, but sometimes, it is because of spiritual misbehavior. Why do some people exhibit paranoia? Because they know that deep down in their hearts they are living in rank disobedience to God. So they spend all their time looking over their shoulders, and well they might! Why do some people engage in irrational behavior? Because they have adopted an irrational position as far as God is concerned, for they profess to know Him, but their hearts are far from Him.

Often, then, there is evidence of psychological disturbance and emotional instability in the lives of those persons who are demonstrating spiritual misbehavior. That is why it is important that we have *Christian* psychologists and psychiatrists. We need counselors who can identify psychological and emotional disturbances and who can also point out when those disturbances have spiritual causes.

Let me offer two cautions. First, do not attribute all emotional and irrational behavior to a spiritual cause. That kind of generalization is grossly out of order. Second, do not assume there is always a natural cause for psychological or emotional imbalance. For it was an evil spirit that came upon Saul from the Lord, and psychological disintegration was certainly a result.

I think the lesson is clear. If you disobey, if you harden your heart to God and go on hardening it, you will not remain emotionally and spiritually unscathed. I believe that with all my heart. One of the greatest abuses of the doctrine of grace has been that some individuals have concluded that God is so gracious and loving that a person can continue disobeying Him with impunity and flaunting His laws without suffering any ramifications. Don't believe that for a minute. I have seen enough of the Scriptures and enough of God's discarded people to know that if we flagrantly disobey and persistently harden our hearts, we cannot come out unscathed. Saul is a salutary reminder to us of this truth.

The church of Jesus Christ needs this message today, possibly as never before.

DAVID AND THE HOLY SPIRIT

Lest you become discouraged by Saul's negative example, let us remember David's expression of the Spirit in contrast to Saul's. One of the servants of Saul said, "I have seen a son of Jesse the Bethlehemite who is skillful in playing, a mighty man of valor, a man of war, prudent in speech, and a handsome person; and [listen to this] the LORD is with him" (1 Sam. 16:18). David's love for God touched the heart of Saul's servant. Saul, despite his deep depression, said, "Send him to me." Why? Because the Spirit of the Lord had come mightily upon David from the very day of his anointing.

And how was this exhibited? They knew that he played the harp well, but it was more than that. When he played that harp, he praised the Lord. That was what they noticed. David was a *worshiper* of God.

Although the Bible does not say it in so many words, I believe that when David played before King Saul he sang the psalms that he had composed as a shepherd boy out on the hills of Bethlehem. He had marveled at the greatness of creation and at God's wondrous grace to human beings. David sang of his experience of the Lord's being his shepherd in the same way that he was a shepherd to the sheep. He sang from the very depths of his being, with praise and honor and glory to God. When he came to Saul and sang, he was found to be a worshiper of God. Often, from seeing their love for God in worship you can tell the men and women on whom the Spirit of God has come to rest.

Besides being a worshiper, David was a courageous warrior. As a boy, he handled a bear and a lion, and God trusted him against Goliath. In other words, the Holy Spirit gives his servants courage. It is the same kind of courage Peter exhibited when he was brought before the Sanhedrin shortly after Pentecost. His courage was not innate, it was a supernatural gift. The Sanhedrin looked at Peter and said, "This is an unlearned man. He's untrained." But he had been with Jesus, and the power of the Holy Spirit was upon him.

The power of the Spirit also enabled David to speak well. A psalmist wrote later on, "My heart is overflowing with a good theme;/ I recite my composition concerning the King,/ My tongue is the pen of a ready writer" (Ps. 45:1). The one on whom the Spirit of God rests sharpens his skills for the glory of God. He is able to declare his experience of God.

Let me ask: When you see the spiritual decline of a soul like that of Saul, doesn't it make your heart tremble? By contrast, when you see someone like David, a man on whom the Spirit of God rested, doesn't it make your heart rejoice? And doesn't it help you tell your heart which way you intend to go in the power of God?

The contrast between the man in spiritual decline and the man in spiritual ascendancy is so stark that we should have no difficulty deciding which way we want to go.

But remember, the way we go is determined by our ongoing relationship with the Spirit of God. We can grieve and quench Him, lie to Him, resist Him, and end up unusable and in despair. Or, we can develop a heart for God— open, malleable, and yielded to Christ. And we will find, like David, a heart full of praise, courage, and skill.

CHAPTER FOUR

A Courageous Heart

The Philistines stood on a mountain on one side, and Israel stood on a mountain on the other side, with a valley between them. And a champion went out from the camp of the Philistines, named Goliath, from Gath, whose height was six cubits and a span. He had a bronze helmet on his head, and he was armed with a coat of mail, and the weight of the coat was five thousand shekels of bronze. And he had bronze greaves on his legs and a bronze javelin between his shoulders. Now the staff of his spear was like a weaver's beam, and his iron spearhead weighed six hundred shekels; and a shield-bearer went before him. Then he stood and cried out to the armies of Israel, and said to them, "Why have you come out to line up for battle?" (1 Sam. 17:3-8).

In one expression in our normal everyday vocabulary we talk about "giant killers." We have in mind, for example, the undersized defensive back in football who beats his larger opposition. One might think of Lech Walesa in Poland. Or, the lone man who takes on city hall and wins. Everybody is thrilled when such a thing happens (unless, of course, they are in city hall!). In our culture we tend to cheer for the underdog, and it is always a delight to see the no-names, the giant killers win.

Something of that attitude appears in 1 Samuel 17 as we read about how David took on Goliath. But although that is certainly one way of looking at the story, we must also recognize there is far more at stake here than just the little man beating the big man. This story is a picture of a greater struggle that is still taking place today, a battle in which you and I are principals. It has a particular message for the church of Jesus Christ today. There is sometimes a lingering hope in all of us that if we can develop a heart for God, somehow the battle will disappear, or at least subside. I would be less than fair if I did not warn you at the outset that it often intensifies. But let us look at the dynamics of the story.

DAVID AND GOLIATH: THE STORY IN CONTEXT

The context of this particular story needs to be clearly understood. The confrontation between David and Goliath was part of a larger struggle between the Philistines and the people of Israel. The struggle between the shepherd boy and the giant needs to be seen on that basis. You will notice, for example, that when David is speaking about Goliath he calls him the "uncircumcised Philistine," not a very complimentary expression.

In Genesis 17:16 we read that one day God spoke to Abraham and told him that his wife Sarah would bear him a son and through his son, he, Abraham, would become the "father of many nations." All nations of the world would be blessed through him. God told Abraham He was making a covenant with Abraham and his people. This covenant was basic: God promised to be their God, and they promised to be His people.

The idea of a covenant is not difficult to understand. I perform the marriage ceremony on a regular basis. The man and woman present themselves and make a covenant with each other. He promises for better or for worse, for richer or for poorer, in sickness and in health, to keep himself only for her and she responds in kind. That is essentially the marriage covenant. When I speak to couples in marital counseling, I always remind them that the *basis* of their relationship is that of a covenant, a mutual commitment, a promise.

God made a covenant with the people of Israel, the children of Abraham: He would be their God and they would be His people. So that they would never forget, He ordained a sign of the covenant: all the males of the nation Israel should be circumcised. This circumcision would be a constant remembrance of the fact that God had entered into a promissory agreement with them.

When David, therefore, called the Philistine giant an "uncircumcised Philistine," he was saying that his opponent did not belong to the covenant people. He was not part of the people of God. In fact, he opposed all that God stood for. Included in that was opposition to God's people. Immediately we see the struggle was not one just between the little guy and the big guy. It was, instead, between the people of God and the people who were not of God.

Not only that, David was particularly upset about something else. He realized that what was going on was a challenge to the authority of "the living God," and he used that expression more than once. The phrase was used in marked contrast to the false gods of whom Goliath spoke. For when Goliath confronted David, he did so by cursing him in the name of his gods.

Just who were those bogus deities? Two of the better-known ones were Dagon and Baal-zebub. Earlier in Israel's history, when the Ark of the Covenant had been captured and placed in the temple of Dagon, the idol of Dagon tumbled down, and the head and hands fell off. The Hebrew literally says, "And only the Dagon was left" (1 Sam. 5:4). The word *dagon* means "fish." Most likely, the god Dagon was a fish god with the head and the hands of a man. It was a grotesque, bizarre mixture of man and fish, this deity that Goliath worshiped. And if that is bizarre, consider Baal-zebub.

Baal literally means "lord," and *Zebub*, "the flies"— "lord of the flies." Even worse, the flies referred to here were popularly called "dung beetles." In other words, the god that the Philistines worshiped had to do with those ghastly beetles that crawled around on excrement and waste.

No wonder David was anxious to meet Goliath's challenge! How would you feel about confronting an enemy who worshiped a weird fish-creature and the god of the flies that crawl on dung? That is the scope, the context, of this encounter. Far more than a little man fighting a big man, it is an account of the people of God being challenged by enemies who snub the living God for the worship of fish and flies.

The word *defy* arises over and over again in this story. The Philistines were aggressively going after the covenant people. They wanted the land that God had given to His people. They intended to get it at any cost. Highly sophisticated and organized, they were also belligerent and arrogant, and they defied the living God. As a result, the relatively disorganized people of Israel were totally demoralized.

Historic accounts of the Philistines at this time tell us they had a virtual corner on the iron market. In fact, there wasn't a single blacksmith in the whole of Israel. When God's people wanted their plows and pruning hooks sharpened, they had to take them down to the Philistines to get the job done. This point may not seem all that important until you realize that if they had no metal and no blacksmiths, they had no swords and no spears. One time when the people of Israel fought the Philistines, they could find only two swords among them—Saul had one and Jonathan had the other. Not only that, but also the Philistines had chariots while the Israelites went everywhere on foot. That is another aspect of the context of the story.

A PICTURE OF THE CHURCH

Because the church of God is likewise under constant attack, we need to understand the context of our battles. And, my friend, they are legion.

For instance, there is an intellectual battle going on for the minds of men and women. We face a tremendous challenge today against the truth as it has been taught traditionally from the Word of God. This challenge is moving into all areas of our culture, and it is a mighty, powerful, and defiant challenge to the people of God, the church. Various people are recognizing the defiance, and some are deciding to do something about it.

In the realm of primary and secondary education, two solutions are being offered. Some have pulled their children out of public schools and established Christian schools. I thoroughly understand that position, and I applaud it. But at the same time, other people are saying, "No, we are going to stay in the public schools and challenge the error where it is taking place." A good friend of mine was recently elected to the local school board, and I applaud that effort as well.

In fact, I don't believe we Christians have the freedom dogmatically to take one of those two positions over the other. Wouldn't Satan love to divide us on that front! What we have to do is recognize that an intellectual battle is going on and get busy—through both the public schools and the Christian schools. Let us take the offense on both fronts and put the enemy to flight. We need to decide whether we are going to allow the Philistines to overcome the covenant people. For heaven's sake, let's not harden our hearts and turn on each other!

A moral battle is also going on for righteousness. Not so long ago, we could look at our traditional moral and ethical norms in America and see a marked similarity between them and biblical ethics. Why? The churches had salted and lighted the culture.

The climate has changed. Sometime ago I was on a live television program. The interviewer said to me, "I would like you to respond to the statement that we in America are now living in the post-Christian era." I used to object to statements like that and say, "They are doomsdayers, born pessimists."

I have changed my mind. We *are* living in a post-Christian era, morally and ethically, in the Western world. Furthermore, we deserve it because of our passivity and by our preoccupation with being "nice" to the morally deviant. A battle is being fought, a tremendous moral and ethical battle. It is a challenge to every piece of truth we have ever stood for. And you know what? The uncircumcised Philistines have the momentum.

In some areas of the world the battle is for downright

physical survival. In recent months I have been in countries where Christians fear for their very lives. This may be a new age for holy martyrs. Some of them are losing their lives for the sake of Jesus Christ. So powerful are the forces arraigned against the people of God that no effective challenge is being made to those defiant forces. It is a fearsome thing. It is not happening in the United States now, but it may. Unless, of course, we are willing to do battle.

The point is, as with David and Goliath, we are not facing a cute story of the lone man against city hall. This is a monumental challenge to the people of God, part of the same challenge that has been going on throughout the centuries.

THE BATTLE OF CHAMPIONS

A significant point about David versus Goliath concerns their manner of fighting. In those days there was a rather interesting approach to settling disputes that saved many lives. Instead of the two armies engaging in battle, each side picked a champion, and the two men fought each other. When the champion won, his whole army was considered to have won.

The Philistines loved that arrangement. They had a man who was over nine feet tall. He led the league in assault and battery. He was superb in battle. And when you have a Goliath on your side, there is no question: you are all in favor of the champion approach to binding settlements. Besides, Israel had a king called Saul who was head and shoulders above everyone else, but he was a coward.

What they all hadn't counted on was a young, wiry, teen-ager, a ruddy-faced kid who spent all his time playing the harp and singing to sheep. He just happened to be on the battlefield that day because his father Jesse had sent him to visit his three older brothers.

When David arrived on the scene, he spotted Goliath. He heard the giant spewing out his defiance and blasphemy.

David's blood began to boil. He looked over in the trenches and could not believe his eyes. All the warriors in his crowd were lying there face down, trying not to be noticed.

What's going on here? David said to himself. *Who's going to champion the cause of the people of God? Who will knock over this uncircumcised Philistine?*

What David was pinpointing for all of us was that individual Christians have to choose whether or not they will champion the cause with which they have chosen to identify. Will they decide to step forward—at the risk of prolonged pain or death—to take their stand? Or will they stay in the trenches? The choice we will make comes down to whether or not we have a heart for God.

We can discuss the physical, moral, and ideological struggles, and talk we must. But the reality of the struggle is an individual Goliath standing for one side against an individual David standing for the other. The people of God have to decide whether they will make the hard choices that the championing of the cause will demand of them.

THE CONTEST

Goliath came out against young David arrogant and defiant, ridiculing and challenging. He had been there forty days and had no takers. Every day that went by he had become more self-confident. Now, some youngster was coming out to meet him, and the boy was not even clad in armor. He didn't even have a sword! Was this some kind of a joke? All this kid had with him was a shepherd's sling. That was it! Goliath roared with laughter. "You come near me little fellow, and I'll tear you limb from limb." He cursed him in the name of his fish and filth gods.

But David didn't flinch. He came right at him. Taking the stone in his hand, he carefully put it in his sling. He whipped it around above his head, and he smote the man mightily in the forehead. Down Goliath tumbled, utterly stunned. David was on him in an instant, taking the giant's sword and decapitating him.

Not only was Goliath overthrown, but the morale of the people of Israel was restored. Victory was accomplished. And that must have been one of the most rewarding moments in the history of the people of God.

Anyone who has been in an athletic contest—or in a business venture or in the military—knows that if morale is at a low ebb, so are results. A key to any contest is the morale.

When it comes to high morale, David could not be touched. But the crucial thing to learn is what *causes* high morale. After all, it is so easy for any of us to become downhearted, especially in the face of what appear to be insurmountable odds. Could it be that morale is connected to having a heart for God?

GETTING IN THE BATTLE

The great concern of a person with a heart for God is to protect the honor of God. David was preoccupied with God's glory, not his own. When the people of God get away from being first concerned about what is best for them and their children and start being concerned for the honor and glory of God Himself, then morale for life returns. It is easy for us believers to become exclusively concerned about what is going to be comfortable and profitable for us. But honoring God is much more important than that.

In fact, it may be that in seeking to glorify God we will get ourselves in situations where things do not turn out all that well for us. Some people in a business situation may be confronted with the fact that a certain stand will be very unprofitable, but that stand will show their concern for the honor and glory of God's name. Things become uncomfortable, unprofitable perhaps, and they may even be fired from the job. But God is glorified.

Somewhere along the line we have to decide whether what we see going on around us is an affront to God's glory. If it is, are we going to sit quietly by and allow it to go on? Or are we going to be a David and say, "Nothing doing!"

You may be asking, "Where do I enter the battle? There are so many things to do."

Here is where you need to discern the will of God. Let me offer some suggestions. First, make the commitment to stand, no matter what. In whatever area God directs you, be sure your heart is soft to do His will, to enter the battle.

Second, survey your own situation. Is there an obvious area where you need to make a stand—at work, at school, in the community? Pray about this. Ask God to speak to you as you read the Scriptures.

Third, Hebrews 13:17 says to be in submission to your spiritual leaders, those who keep watch over your soul. Seek out your pastor. Ask him if he can spot any area where the Lord could use you on the spiritual battlefront. He might have been praying for a volunteer just like you.

Let me tell you—the Christian life is exciting! What a privilege it is to be used by God in the service of Christ's church!

THREE PRACTICAL NOTES

In a final review of David's victory over Goliath, let me mention three observations which, I think, will help your staying power in the battles you face.

1. Don't look for automatic applause from fellow believers.

Sometimes, when we sense we are in God's will, we assume that everyone else will feel that way too and rejoice. Not so!

Just when David was ready to answer Goliath's challenge, a nasty thing happened to him. Yet he came out of the problem stronger than before. What happened? He was reprimanded by his older brother Eliab. And the situation was very difficult for him.

There David was—his sights set on Goliath—trying to rouse the people of God. He was only a young person trying to help Saul put some backbone in the place of his wishbone, and get the Israelite soldiers up out of the bottom of their trenches so that they could take some positive action. He was all set to challenge Goliath.

Without any warning, his older brother Eliab angrily said, "What are you doing here anyway? I'll bet you didn't even make provision for those puny sheep you're supposed to be looking after. I know what's wrong with you—you've got a bad heart. You're an opportunist, here to be Mr. Big Man against Goliath. Now get out of here and go home!"

What happened as far as David was concerned was that he said, "Well, what's the matter with you?" Then he did a very wise thing. He turned away and got on with it.

One of the things that will invariably happen to people who obey God is that sometimes a fellow Christian will become their biggest opposition. Try to be like David and ask, "Hey, listen, what's the problem?" Then try to sort the thing out if you can, turn away from it, and get on with doing God's will.

2. Keep it simple.

The second thing you will notice about this contest is that the strategy was sublimely simple. What happened to Goliath? A little stone sent from a sling hit him in the forehead. How much more basic can you get?

I used to read that story and wonder how a little shot from a sling could do so much damage—until one day in Bethany near Jerusalem I came across a little shepherd boy. He had a sling. He picked up some stones from the road and started to sling this thing around and around in a circle above his head. It was going so fast it was a blur, and you could hear it whirring. Then he let the stone go. It went like a shot out of a rifle. Crack! I'll tell you something, I would not like to have been Mr. Goliath! David's strategy was to size up the opposition quickly and go straight for it. Simply. Decisively. Don't complicate the carrying out of God's will.

3. Never adopt the enemy's methods.

The thing in David's favor was that he was quick, young, and mobile. The liability of Goliath was his size: big, clumsy, and immobile. But his method of fighting was what everybody expected in such a battle, and Saul thought he should equip David with Philistine weapons. But in doing that he would have taken away the natural assets God had given David. There is a lesson for us here.

Sometimes in our desire to take on the forces that are arraigned against us, we decide we need to use the same methods—their same armor. We don't. God equips and arms us.

During the hippie years, I recall watching a young Christian man trying to reach the counterculture people for Christ. He became a plastic hippie to do it. They would scream; he would scream. They would demonstrate; he would demonstrate. Do you know what? He lost. The people who were successful were those who learned to give soft answers that turn away wrath, a blessing for a curse, love for hatred.

Keep spiritual. Keep practical. Don't allow yourself to be bogged down with a method that might become the means of making sure you don't achieve your end. Look for the weakness of your opponent and aggressively pursue it in the power of the living God.

If the Davids of this world are the champions of the people of God, the Goliaths are the champions of the opponents of God. Only people who have real morale, real strategy, and real expertise can take on the big ones—people with a heart for God. Be patient and mature. May God grant that we produce these kinds of champions in our churches.

CHAPTER FIVE

On Becoming
a Friend

And it was so, when he had finished speaking to Saul, that the soul of Jonathan was knit to the soul of David, and Jonathan loved him as his own soul. Saul took him that day, and would not let him go home to his father's house anymore. Then Jonathan and David made a covenant, because he loved him as his own soul. And Jonathan took off the robe that was on him and gave it to David, with his armor, even to his sword and his bow and his belt.

So David went out wherever Saul sent him, and behaved wisely. And Saul set him over the men of war, and he was accepted in the sight of all the people and also in the sight of Saul's servants. Now it had happened as they were coming home, when David was returning from the slaughter of the Philistine, that the women had come out of all the cities of Israel, singing and dancing, to meet King Saul, with tambourines, with joy, and with musical instruments. So the women sang as they danced, and said:

"Saul has slain his thousands,
And David his ten thousands."

Then Saul was very angry, and the saying displeased him; and he said, "They have ascribed to David ten thousands, and to me they have ascribed but thousands. Now what more can he have but the kingdom?" So Saul eyed David from that day forward.

And it happened on the next day that the distressing spirit from God came upon Saul, and he prophesied inside the house. So David played music with his hand, as at other times; but there was a spear in Saul's hand. And Saul cast the spear, for he said, "I will pin David to the wall with it." But David escaped his presence twice.

Now Saul was afraid of David, because the LORD was with him, but had departed from Saul. Therefore Saul removed him from his presence, and made him his captain over a thousand; and he went out and came in before the people. And David behaved wisely in all his ways, and the LORD was with him. Therefore, when Saul saw that he behaved very wisely, he was afraid of him. But all Israel and Judah loved David, because he went out and came in before them

(1 Sam. 18:1-16).

W hen we talk about each individual Christian's developing a heart for God, we do not mean learning to go it alone with Him. Godliness is not being isolated and independent from other Christians.

The youngest son among eight, David began his career by looking after a few sheep in the hills of Judea outside of Bethlehem. Then he became a favorite in the court of King Saul. Everything seemed to be going his way.

But then a dramatic change took place. We see a marked deterioration in the fortunes of David. His life became increasingly tension filled.

It is beautiful to see how the support he needed came from an unexpected source. None other than King Saul's son and heir, Jonathan, would become a close personal friend of David. At great personal risk and considerable inconvenience, he accepted full responsibility for David's care. This story is a wonderful example of what it means to experience the fullness of fellowship between friends. It can be applied not only in terms of our individual relationship with the Lord, but also in terms of genuine human friendships—and particularly the fellowship that one can reasonably expect to enjoy in the church of Jesus Christ.

AN EMERGING NEED

After David killed Goliath and instilled confidence in the disorganized and demoralized soldiers of the army of Israel, a great victory was won over the Philistines. The Israelites came back and were greeted by singing and dancing. But one sour note was inadvertently sounded.

The Scripture says that as they welcomed King Saul, they sang, "Saul has slain his thousands,/And David his ten thousands" (1 Sam. 18:7).

Saul realized it was necessary to have David in a position of considerable leadership in his army. The officers agreed with this judgment, and David's popularity led to promotion. His respect was well deserved.

David acted wisely; he performed creditably. Depending on the Lord, he did what he firmly believed was God's will. Matching his considerable skills with his dependence upon the Lord, David became remarkably prosperous. In spite of all these positive things, however, he was introduced to a whole new set of problems.

The main problem, of course, was Saul. He couldn't handle all the notoriety being heaped upon David. Sad to say, David found in Saul his chief enemy. The king became dangerous and difficult.

David's acceptance by the people in general made Saul extremely angry. It began with the song the people sang when the men returned from the battle. I have no doubt they were trying to compliment the troops, but it failed as far as Saul was concerned. It was probably an antiphonal song where half the crowd would sing, "Saul has slain his thousands," and the other half would respond, "and David his ten thousands."

You can feel the impact. This message penetrated to the marrow of Saul's bones. He couldn't handle the comparison being made between him and David.

Further, it was probably dawning on Saul that all was not well within him. God's removal of His Spirit from Saul and His anointing of David were beginning to show. Before both God and the people, Saul must have begun to sense that his star was waning.

COMPETITORS—BEWARE!

Many of us can identify with this kind of situation because we have been threatened by what is happening in our relationships with other people. It is not uncommon in the business community to get a promotion at somebody else's expense. With the promotion, you are going to promote a new problem. In fact, you usually can't have the promotion without the problem. Having a heart for God means you will not flaunt your success, but you will try to understand and bring peace into the situation.

David's sheer attractiveness made Saul afraid. There was a charisma about this young shepherd boy that was absolutely undeniable. And I suppose that fact came home most forcibly to Saul when he found that his own daughter had fallen in love with David, too. It perhaps seemed to Saul that *everybody* was in love with David.

Saul made some genuine attempts to get along with David. Quite often we see a magnanimous spirit coming through in Saul. He tried to rectify matters, but it didn't work. You have to feel sorry for Saul because he tried to bear David, but he couldn't, and he tried to beat him, but he couldn't. Eventually he tried to destroy him, but he couldn't do that either. It was an exercise in sheer frustration.

"So Saul eyed David from that day forward" (1 Sam. 18:9). Saul realized his days were numbered, and he became insanely jealous.

One of the worst things that can happen to us in the sensitive area of the human spirit is to find a competitor with whom we can't compete. Be careful—it will happen to you. And when it does, tremendous frustration, envy, and jealousy can build up. It will do terrible, terrible damage to you unless there is a mighty work of the Spirit of God there, casting out the envy and the jealousy. If you go into the situation with a heart to obey God, to bow to the other person's talent, you will act appropriately. If a root of bitterness springs up, remove it at once.

Saul's deep-rooted jealousy turned into outright hostility. First Samuel 18:19, for instance, illustrates one such hostile act. Saul had promised his older daughter in marriage to David. At the last minute, when David expected to be married, the king gave his daughter to someone else. What a terrible thing to do. But this was the kind of treatment that David received from the jealous, antagonistic King Saul.

Then, Saul told David to go out and bring in evidence he had killed one hundred Philistines (see v. 25). If he did that feat, he would be allowed to marry Saul's number two daughter. But Saul's plan was never to give him the second daughter nor to see him win a victory over the Philistines. The idea was simply to get David killed. Later on, when Saul realized his second daughter had fallen in love with David, he could not cope with the fact. He remained David's enemy for the rest of his days.

Remember, only a very short time had elapsed since David was quietly, happily, looking after his sheep in the Judean wilderness behind his home in Bethlehem. Through nothing of his own doing, he was chosen by God and anointed by Samuel. He was only doing what he understood to be right when he challenged Goliath and defeated him. He had a dramatic rise, but he made a mortal enemy. And his life was in terrible danger.

And that is how it is, fellow Christians. When you set out to develop a heart for God, to serve Christ and His church no matter what, it is not unusual to find a whole new set of problems—problems that were never expected, things they never told you in school or in seminary. We may not understand, we may have no way of knowing, why they come about. It may be that in some instances we are responsible. But often we are not. God is simply allowing it to see if we still mean business! That was David's dilemma.

THE NEED IS MET

God had a beautiful provision for David at the time of his perplexity. It was a special friendship—with none other than King Saul's eldest son, Jonathan.

There are three things that stand out very forcibly concerning that friendship. First Samuel 18:1 says, "The soul of Jonathan was knit to the soul of David, and Jonathan loved him as his own soul." "Then Jonathan and David made a covenant because he loved him as his own soul" (v. 3). Note these three phrases: (1) The soul of Jonathan was knit to the soul of David; (2) Jonathan and David made a covenant; and (3) Jonathan loved David as his own soul. Those are the three key characteristics of any friendship.

SOUL BROTHERS

David and Jonathan had many qualities in common. That is why they became one in spirit. The literal translation here is very interesting. What it actually says in 1 Samuel 18:1 is "the soul of Jonathan was chained with the soul of David." Soul brothers! In other words, the inner man of Jonathan was bound, as it were, with chains and linked inextricably with the inner man of David.

The simple fact of the matter is that where there is to be a strong relationship of friendship, there has to be soul chained to soul. But what were these things they had in common? Let's mention a few of them.

1. True piety

We are first introduced to Jonathan in 1 Samuel 14. We read that Jonathan had decided the Philistines were getting away with far too much. He took the initiative with his armorbearer to test whether the Lord would deliver the whole of the hosts of the Philistines into their hands.

"Nothing," he said, "restrains the LORD from saving, by many or by few" (1 Sam. 14:6).

Jonathan had a tremendous sense of trust in the Lord. He and his armorbearer took on the whole host of the Philistines because Jonathan was firmly convinced that if God was involved, nothing could stop them. But if God was not involved, it wouldn't matter if they had twenty thousand men—they still couldn't win.

Jonathan was utterly and totally convinced of the power of God. It comes as no surprise, therefore, to discover that Jonathan was immediately attracted to David. For in response to Goliath's challenging the armies of Israel, the young shepherd boy said, "The battle is the Lord's," which sounds very similar to what Jonathan said.

2. Humility

Saul was completely threatened by David's popularity, and he said so. But when Jonathan talked about the same subject to David, he said, " '...You shall be king over Israel, and I shall be next to you' " (1 Sam. 23:17). That was the heir to the throne talking!

As far as Jonathan was concerned, the Lord would save, the Lord would act, and nobody would hinder Him. That attitude spilled over into a humble dependence upon the Lord to work in his life, whether he was king or whether David was king. Whether Jonathan was number one or number two was irrelevant to him.

You will find the same attitude in David. When David was told by the king that he could marry his daughter, he said, "I'm a poor man, I have no dowry." He was saying, "No way could I ever marry the king's daughter." Humility.

3. Duty

When Jonathan saw the armies of the Philistines sitting around doing nothing, he grabbed his armorbearer, and the two of them opposed all the Philistines. When David saw Goliath and the army of the Philistines and then observed Israel's men hiding in the bottom of their trenches, quaking for fear, he took charge. Because both David and Jonathan had a clear sense of duty, they were prepared to follow that path of duty.

4. Loyalty

In the end David had to run for his life. Notice what Jonathan did. One would anticipate that he would have gone with David. But he didn't—he chose to remain with his father, King Saul. Why? Because he was enamored of his father? No. He stayed with Saul because he believed that his father needed him more than David did. That's very interesting because later on when David, for fear of his life as Saul chased him, had the opportunity on more than one occasion to kill Saul, he backed off. You see, they both had a deep sense of loyalty to this demented king.

When you come across two people who have a deep sense of mutual loyalty, piety, humility, and duty, you have the potential to see two souls linked together. When people have those noble virtues in common, they have the stuff of which a powerful liaison can be made and a friendship that is stronger than death. David described his friendship with Jonathan as "surpassing the love of women" (2 Sam. 1:26). It was a friendship based on mutual qualities that they deeply admired in each other, and for which they thanked God.

Do you see the secret here? What produced these similar qualities in the two men was that *they both possessed a heart for God. The secret in lasting friendship is not simply to find someone like yourself. It is to develop a heart for God and then seek out others who love Him, too.*

One of the greatest strengths for Christendom at this present hour would be for people to recognize those qualities in other people and in themselves and find their hearts chained together. Imagine building bonds of friendship upon those qualities! Think what kind of a marriage you could have if your soul was knit—chained and fettered—with another person who was like that. Think what the church of Jesus Christ would be if we built teams of people with these qualities in common. We have work to do, haven't we?

A COVENANT RELATIONSHIP

A covenant like the one David and Jonathan shared was very common in the Old Testament. Sometimes it was a political treaty; one nation would make a compact with another. Other times it was a working contract; labor would make an agreement with management. Or it was a religious vow; God would stake His reputation on a commitment to His people.

In the case here, it was a pact of friendship. But the same word is used to describe all of these ideas.

And the idea, of course, was one of strong commitment. One nation made a commitment to another to behave in a certain way. A class of people in a work agreement promised to deliver certain goods, and the other party promised to remunerate them in a certain way. In a religious vow, God took the initiative by promising to be their God, and the people responded by saying, "And we will be Your people." There is a deep sense of promise, commitment, and loyalty. And the covenant was the root of the relationship.

The initiative for this friendship pact between David and Jonathan came from Prince Jonathan. That is quite significant when you think about the differences in their social status. And later, when David was in a position of need for an ally in the palace, Jonathan proved loyal to his commitment even to the point of protecting David from King Saul's murderous plans. It was a genuine act of love and loyalty, initiated by one who had the power to help his friend. One very important lesson to remember is you cannot choose who your loyal friends will be. You can choose to *be* a friend, but not to *have* a friend. Your friends will choose to be your friends. You cannot operate from the basis of need and demand their attention. You can operate from the basis of supply and offer yourself to the area of need. If Jonathan was not interested in being to David what he needed, nothing that David could have said or done would have helped.

In common with the custom of that time, Jonathan gave gifts to David: his armor, some of his clothes, and even his sword. Remember, swords were in short supply at that particular time. But he was given the opportunity of dressing in the armor of the prince. And when he went into battle, he held the sword of none other than the heir to the throne. This was tangible evidence of the friendship.

The applications for us are legion. For instance, the Prince of Glory took the initiative and came down to this world to us and made an offer of friendship and communion—a commitment of Himself to you. By His death He gave tangible evidence of His loyalty to the covenant, and He sealed it with His blood.

Is your understanding of friendship and fellowship such that you have taken the initiative in building relationships? And in taking the initiative, have you made lasting commitments with people? Once you have identified people with whom you share things in common, give them evidence of your commitment to them. Once you have done that, you will find many of them responding and reciprocating.

The Scriptures say, "A man who has friends must himself be friendly,/But there is a friend who sticks closer than a brother" (Prov. 18:24). Don't ever say, "Nobody cares about me. Nobody is interested." When people see you are a person who takes the initiative, builds relationships, and invests himself or herself in other people, then friendship and loyalty to the commitment will be reciprocated.

A SENSE OF COMMUNION

Jonathan loved David as he loved himself.

One of the sickening opinions in our contemporary society is that some people have identified theirs as a homosexual relationship. Clearly, people who would reach such a conclusion and use it as a rationale for homosexual behavior are in total defiance of the heart of the Scriptures, and those individuals are thereby making public a personal commentary on their own twisted minds. Not the slightest shred of evidence exists of any impropriety of a sexual nature in this relationship.

What we see in truth is a noble, glorious friendship that is deeply spiritual, deeply manly, absolutely superb in all qualities. The fact that Scripture says that Jonathan loved David more than himself reflects the commandment of God, that we should love God with all our hearts and our neighbor as ourselves.

Jonathan took seriously those commands. But when we say he loved David as himself, what does that mean? You can point to several things. It was a love that transcended differences of rank. The prince loved the shepherd boy. It was a love that accepted all manner of danger and risk. Jonathan went constantly into the presence of David's arch enemy, King Saul, and interceded on David's behalf. It was a love that insisted upon speaking the truth. When it was necessary to speak out as a matter of conviction—whether Jonathan to David, David to Jonathan, or Jonathan to Saul—this action was a part of that love. It was a selfless love that reached to the point of deepest need.

FINDING FRIENDS

For those of us who are Christians, that friend who sticks closer than a brother is our Lord Jesus Christ. Be sure your relationship is *there*, solid and settled. Give complete control of your life to Him, both once and for all and daily.

Then, turn your attention to developing earthly friendships. Examine the qualities of your life. What qualities do you have that other people would find they want to have in common with you? For what good reasons should they be responsive to you? What initiatives are you taking? If you would have friends, you must show yourself friendly. Reach out to people, not to advance your position, but to advance their condition.

Finally, when it comes to the fellowship of believers in the church, what kinds of commonness do you have with other believers? Who are the Christians with whom you spend time? Are they committed to Christ in His body, the church?

You say, "Well, I don't have anybody. Nobody has shown any interest in me." Turn that around and ask yourself, "What initiatives have I taken to look out for people?" Men, particularly, I ask you this question. David and Jonathan's story is one about men, manly faith, masculine courage, male love. Are you reaching out to other men? Sink down lasting roots with other men in your church.

I hear repeatedly, "Aw, I stopped going to that church." "Why?"

"I didn't get anything out of it."

"Well, is that why you went—to get something out of it? I thought we went to put something into it! Service. Worship. Friendship."

"Well, I don't get involved in that sort of thing anymore."

"Why not?"

"It doesn't meet my needs."

"Hey, wait. You go as a Jonathan to find a David to address *his* needs."

What happened to the commitment you made to your church or to your spouse? To those children? You see, the stuff of which spiritual life is made is communion with Christ and with people who share a heart for God, building up the things we have in common. David, at the hour of his greatest need, found a divine provision in the prince who took the initiative of commitment and communion and ministered to him.

Our Lord Jesus has demonstrated the same thing to us. What He asks us is, In what way are we responding to Him and taking initiatives for befriending others? I urge you, be one of God's answers in terms of fellowship and friendship with other people.

CHAPTER SIX

The Clear-Channel Conscience

And David said in his heart, "Now I shall perish someday by the hand of Saul. There is nothing better for me than that I should speedily escape to the land of the Philistines; and Saul will despair of me, to seek me anymore in any part of Israel. So I shall escape out of his hand." Then David arose and went over with the six hundred men who were with him to Achish the son of Maoch, king of Gath. So David dwelt with Achish at Gath, he and his men, each man with his household, and David with his two wives, Ahinoam the Jezreelitess, and Abigail the Carmelitess, Nabal's widow. And it was told Saul that David had fled to Gath; so he sought him no more.

Then David said to Achish, "If I have now found favor in your eyes, let them give me a place in some town in the country, that I may dwell there. For why should your servant dwell in the royal city with you?" So Achish gave him Ziklag that day. Therefore Ziklag has belonged to the kings of Judah to this day. Now the time that David dwelt in the country of the Philistines was one full year and four months.

And David and his men went up and raided the Geshurites, the Girzites, and the Amalekites. For those nations were the inhabitants of the land from of old, as you go to Shur, even as

far as the land of Egypt. Whenever David at-
tacked the land, he left neither man nor woman
alive, but took away the sheep, the oxen, the
donkeys, the camels, and the apparel, and returned and came to Achish. Then Achish would
say, "Where have you made a raid today?" And
David would say, "Against the southern area of
Judah, or against the southern area of the Jerah-
meelites, or against the southern area of the
Kenites." David would save neither man nor
woman alive, to bring news to Gath, saying,
"Lest they should inform on us, saying, 'Thus
David did.' " And so was his behavior all the
time he dwelt in the country of the Philistines.
So Achish believed David, saying, "He has made
his people Israel utterly abhor him; therefore he
will be my servant forever" (1 Sam. 27:1-12).

Hand in hand with possessing a heart for God is learning the proper use of conscience. Three separate instances in David's life provide us with a valuable look at the human conscience and how to keep it clear and clean. In David's case, two of these instances showed improper use of conscience, while a third exhibited godliness. But we learn from all three.

A DEFINITION

Conscience, as the word itself suggests, is that part of us that "knows alongside"—*con*, "with or alongside," and *science*, "to know, to know with." Both the Latin and Greek languages give us this same concept.

A part of our minds knows *facts*, and a moral part of us knows what is the *right* or *wrong* thing to do with those facts. It is one thing to have the facts; it is an entirely different thing to know right from wrong concerning those facts.

God has given us both the ability to have data punched into our system—our mind—and a conscience that enables us to sort out right and wrong. We are designed to make moral choices before we engage in an action. Conscience will tell us what is right or wrong before and after we engage in the action.

THE CARE AND FEEDING OF THE HUMAN CONSCIENCE

Conscience, however, needs to be carefully maintained because it can become desensitized. And conscience can be abused. Paul said it can be "seared with a hot iron" (1 Tim. 4:2). In the same way that we brand cattle or horses, burning into the flesh and blunting the nerve endings, so we can desensitize our conscience. If we are not careful, in this searing process of the conscience, it can cease to speak to us about what is right and wrong.

Conscience also needs to be educated. Conscience has the natural ability to differentiate between right and wrong, but it needs to be programmed as to what is right and wrong according to divine revelation. It is important that we recognize this fact.

When I was preaching in Singapore some time ago, we were preparing to sing the first hymn on the first night of the meetings. They had a piano and an organ, and both began playing the hymn in the key of C. But they were at least a tone and a half away from each other. They were on target as far as the keyboards were concerned. But one was tuned in one key and one in another.

The songleader turned to the organist and whispered, "This is in the key of C."

"That's what I'm playing," the organist said.

Then the songleader went over to the pianist, "This is the key of C."

She said, "That's what I'm playing, too."

They were both functioning as directed. But it was obvious that one, if not both, was wrong.

Sometimes conscience, with its function to say what is right and wrong, will say, "What is being done here is correct," but by God's standard it is not. In the same way, the piano or organ keyboard can be intact, but if it isn't tuned properly, it may look right and be all wrong. Jiminy Cricket was wrong! Conscience can't always be your guide. Conscience must be tuned to the orthodoxy of Christian faith in order to be your proper guide. With these things in mind, let's look at the three incidents in the life of David and see what we can learn from them.

CONSCIENCE AND SOCIAL CONSENSUS

David already had a wife, but he took a second one—Abigail, the widow of Nabal. He engaged in polygamy, or multiple marriage. Here is a classic example of somebody quieting his conscience because he accepted the consensus of the society around him.

From the very beginning of time, God said clearly, "Therefore a man shall leave his father and mother and be joined to his wife, and they shall become one flesh" (Gen. 2:24). David could not say he was living according to that command, because there were three of them—and three cannot become one!

In a society that did not know God, polygamy was a normal procedure. It was perfectly acceptable and, unfortunately, the people of God had decided it was acceptable to them as well. They simply ignored what God said and went along with the social consensus.

Can you picture this conversation? "David, do you know that God says, 'For this cause shall a man leave his father and mother and cleave to his wife, and they too shall be one flesh'?"

"Sure."

"Well, how do you account for what you're doing? You've got two wives."

David would probably have said, "But everybody's doing it. It's just the normal thing." Israelite society had slid into an acceptance of her neighbors' behavior on this point, and David simply went along with common practice.

Be sobered by the reality that we are all very susceptible to feeding our consciences with the consensus of those around us, all the while carefully ignoring or even convincing ourselves that it goes along with what God has said. And in doing that, you can quiet your conscience. Let me give you an example.

A general attitude concerning sexual morality in our modern society is not in keeping with what God has said. We all know that. Anybody who is aware of the social consensus today concerning sexual morality, and who knows what God says, recognizes there is no similarity whatsoever between the two. Our society has chloroformed its conscience as far as God's Word on this point is concerned.

The terrible thing is that many of the people of God have done exactly the same thing. Too frequently we come across Christian people who, as far as sexual morality is concerned, are also light years away from what God has said. And they have no conscience about it at all. When they are confronted, they often get upset and say, "You're interfering. Everybody is doing it."

One of the great dangers to us in our Christian experience is we may be so submerged by the social consensus that our conscience is dulled concerning what God has said.

Another example. The Bible teaches quite clearly that Christians should adopt a sacrificial lifestyle; they should recognize that all they are and all they have are the Lord's. Society as a whole says, "That's crazy! All you have is yours. You worked for it, you've got it, you do what you like with it." Some people of God have desensitized their consciences concerning giving, making only token gifts to the Lord. They have gone along with the cultural consensus, "What I have is mine."

Or, on another issue, the Scriptures teach the sanctity of human life, but our society murders a million unborn human beings each year. It would be easy to offer many more similar illustrations. Either we tune our own consciences to the Word of God, or we accept the social consensus. We must make that choice.

CONSCIENCE AND CONVICTION

Next, we see an entirely different side of David. Here is the use of conscience concerning conviction.

David was confronted with an opportunity to get rid of his archenemy, Saul. But David refused to lift up a hand against "the Lord's anointed." He walked away from his opportunity, as he had already done once before. He had strong convictions about God's authority in the king's office built into his conscience, and on that point he acted nobly. Consensus was not governing his conscience; it was God's conviction at work. The situation happened this way.

One evening, David was looking over the camp of Israel. Everyone had fallen asleep. Right in the center of the camp was King Saul in deep slumber, and all his bodyguards were asleep around him. David and one of his young men went down into the camp and picked their way through all the sleeping bodies, right to the side of Saul. David's companion said, "Let me finish him off. I'll only need one shot. I promise you I won't need to strike him twice."

But David said no. His convictions molded his conscience. He knew that God held him accountable for his actions.

One of the great difficulties Christian people encounter today is that when it comes to a matter of hard, directive decisions they rarely have built-in, combat-ready conviction. There is a vacuum concerning what God says and often no thought of a God who is to be feared. And tragically, there is little thought today of a God who is to be worshiped. Christians, *our* consciences may have become chloroformed.

David, at this point, was right on target. His convictions concerning God had him in tune with truth. His conscience was working beautifully. To disobey the Lord concerning Saul would have propelled him into a very proper sense of guilt.

There are, of course, two kinds of guilt—true guilt and false guilt. Christian psychologists have helped us with differentiating between the two.

1. False guilt

False guilt arises when unrealistic expectations are laid upon us—expectations for which we are completely inadequate, demands we just can't handle. This guilt sometimes appears in childhood. Unrealistic parents will place an intolerable load upon their child. The child will grow up bearing this burden and become very discouraged and disgruntled. Children will decide they are completely inadequate and may engage in all kinds of behavior that shows they just can't cope. They are made to feel guilty, and they carry false guilt later into their marriages. This guilt becomes imposed upon their spouses and their children, and all hell breaks loose.

However, it must also be said that in many instances psychologists have been considerably less than helpful to us in distinguishing false guilt from true guilt. Once they have identified false guilt, some go on to assume that *all* guilt is false. They ignore the fact that there is also such a thing as true guilt.

2. True guilt

True guilt makes itself known when I stand before God justly condemned. At that particular point if I don't listen to my guilt, my conscience begins to be seared with that hot iron, and I am in difficulty.

I find some Christian people confusing the two. For instance, sometimes as I talk with a person about a certain spiritual obligation, he or she will say to me, "Stuart, don't lay a guilt trip on me. Don't try to make me feel guilty. I can't handle it. I've got enough problems without your cornering me."

As a pastor, a minister of the glorious gospel of Christ, do I have the right to talk with people about giving, about getting into ministry, about being accountable in the church? I should hope so! Biblically, historically, this has always been a vital part of the pastor's role. And we dare not lose this prerogative.

But sometimes, in fact disconcertingly frequently, people react with, "Don't you try to make me feel guilty." If I am deliberately trying to make them feel guilty, that is not biblical, then false guilt comes and I am wrong. If, on the other hand, I am simply teaching a clearly scriptural principle, applying it to their lives, and giving them the opportunity to make a righteous response, and they refuse and feel guilty, hallelujah! So they should! The simple fact of the matter is if we do not obey God when we have the opportunity, that disobedience is *sin*.

Disobedience is sin, and sin means you are guilty. Condemned. If you stand condemned before a fearsome and awesome God, the worst thing a pastor can do is let you off the hook. Then *I* sin. No, when sin leads to guilt, the best thing that can happen is to admit it and ask for forgiveness. This is what the writer to the Hebrews calls "having our hearts sprinkled from an evil conscience" (Heb. 10:22).

Thus, there is a huge difference between false guilt and true guilt. False guilt is produced by the unrealistic expectations laid upon you by someone else, or even yourself, quite apart from what God says. True guilt comes from knowing that God has told you to do something and you don't do it; that's sin, disobedience, and you are guilty. You stand condemned and you need to confess the sin and be forgiven.

David, in refusing to murder Saul, had a clear understanding concerning God's will.

CONVICTION VERSUS COINCIDENCE

David had clear convictions not only about God and

about guilt but also about grace. When David went into the camp and saw Saul and all the soldiers asleep, he realized it was an abnormal situation. First Samuel 26:12 says the *Lord* had put them into "a deep sleep." In other words, David identified this circumstance as some kind of divine intervention. He was sensitive to God. In the affairs of life, David had come to know that it was possible for God to intervene in unusual and dramatic ways. And when He did, David perceived it as an evidence of God's grace. God had provided for him there the opportunity to do right! Another chance to eschew evil and minister to Saul.

You see, it is possible to so deaden a conscience concerning God that one loses all sight of God's gracious intervention in life. If that is the case, such a person will simply go on rationalizing every event as totally unrelated to God. This rationalizing is precisely why so many miss much of what God has in store for them. Everything becomes coincidence.

One remarkable "coincidence" for David was when he got back to Ziklag and found it burned down (see 1 Sam. 30). All the people and property had been taken away. He had no idea who did it. But David's group happened to bump into an Egyptian, the slave of an Amalekite, who knew about the matter and was prepared to do something about it. It was one of those "coincidences" that, as the whole story evolved, was obviously a gracious provision of God.

There are some people who would shrug their shoulders and say, "Another coincidence, so what?" Others who are sensitive to what God is doing in the so-called coincidences of life are so attuned to His working out His purposes that they are prepared to recognize His grace at work.

Just before that incident, as David had marched proudly with his six hundred men as the bodyguard of the Philistines, he found that all the commanders of the rest of the troops were against him. They talked to King Achish and said, "Get rid of that David. We don't need him. He could be our Achilles' heel. His sympathies are with Saul. Remember, he's the man who killed Goliath, he's the one of whom they sing, 'Saul has killed his thousands, but David his ten thousands.' Don't forget those ten thousands were our people! Get him out of here."

David was utterly humiliated by the whole thing. He was flatly rejected by everybody, and they immediately dismissed him. But very quickly he was glad for that opposition. If it hadn't been for his enemies, he would not have returned to Ziklag in time to follow the people who had raided his home and taken his wives and children. Here again, David saw the grace of God, even in an adverse situation.

It is not uncommon to find that God's people have become so insensitive to His promptings, and so insensitive to guilt, that they are utterly insensitive to His grace, too. They operate purely on the basis of visible facts, without the benefit of a conscience in tune with God to enable them to interpret those facts correctly. God help us when that happens.

CONVENIENCE

A third example of how David used his conscience can be seen in his decision to escape from Saul by going to live among the Philistines. In making such a move, he was handling his conscience on the basis of convenience. This is another classic way of blunting the conscience for the sake of what is comfortable. He made a big decision recorded for us in 1 Samuel 27. His decision was, "I'm worn out with living in the wilderness. I've had it up to here with trying to outrun Saul. I need a break. I know what I'll do—I'll join the Philistines. Saul won't dare come and chase me. I'll get him off my back, and I can have some peace."

He contravened God's instructions. As a man of God,

David had no right to identify himself with the enemies of God. Further, it was a decision that ignored past experience. He had been down there once before (see 1 Sam. 21:10-15). Remember? He got in the house of Achish, and when they suddenly recognized him (which wasn't surprising because he dragged Goliath's sword with him), he feigned madness. He let saliva dribble down his beard. He scratched on the door. Achish said, "I've got enough crazy men around here. I don't need another." And they kicked him out.

David's behavior contradicted not only God's will but also what David himself believed. Look at the psalms he wrote about God's defending him! Why would anybody in his right mind make a volitional decision that would contradict what God has said? The answer is surprisingly easy. Instead of listening to what our conscience is telling us, we are more concerned with what is convenient and comfortable for us.

When David got down to where the Philistines were, guess what! He was warmly accepted. In his own country he was hounded like a pheasant in the wilderness. His own people didn't want him. They chased him from pillar to post. They were after his life. But the enemies of God embraced him.

I have met many believers who, when they have been confronted with their sin, leave in a huff. They turn away from God's people and take up with the enemy. You talk with them about their adultery and what they are doing with their marriages, and instead of listening to what God says, they accept what is convenient for themselves. They tell me, "I found more acceptance in a singles bar than I did in the church of Jesus Christ."

Of course they did. Because in the church of Jesus Christ we are not called to tell people what they want to hear. Instead we attempt to sensitize the conscience to what God says, and sometimes that hurts.

With the Philistines, David not only found a great sense of acceptance, he also had peace. Deep peace. Finally, Saul left him alone.

How many times have you heard of situations when people are confronted with right and wrong and they glibly ignore it and say, "Well, I've got peace about it." I want to tell you something. You *can* have immediate peace about your sin. You can feel extremely comfortable and warmly accepted in your disobedience. But never for one moment assume that because you have peace about it and are accepted by others that it is right. What you have is a deadened conscience.

The lady playing the piano in Singapore was playing in the key of C; she knew she was right. The lady playing the organ in the key of C knew she was right. There was only one problem. One of them—perhaps both—was not tuned in the key of C.

A HAPPY ENDING

Fortunately we can end on a happy note. The end of our story shows David once again salvaging the situation, which is what made him a man after God's own heart. Let me reiterate. He was not a man after God's own heart because he was perfect. He was a man after God's own heart because, in his imperfection, he had a longing to be righteous and a readiness to work on it.

David again called the priest to bring the ephod and hear what God had to say. Here we go again. Here was the man after God's own heart.

As I have studied this passage of Scripture, it has spoken deeply to my own heart. I have been deeply convicted of how easy it is for me to quiet my conscience, to put it out of gear, and to be concerned with the general consensus for what is convenient.

I can so easily turn away from the whole thing, simply shrug my shoulders and say, "That's how it is," thereby proving that I am not a man after God's own heart. Or, I can humbly confess what I am, what I have done, and say to the Lord, "I have a conscience here that is not clear before You. I confess it, dear Lord, it troubles me deeply. I ask You once again, Father, to apply that precious blood of our Lord Jesus to this unclean conscience of mine, and forgive me. Cleanse me, and give me renewal and refreshment, that I might be what You want me to be."

May I ask you something? Is that what you want? Are you prepared to identify yourself with the host of heaven and say, "Oh, God, there's one thing I want more than any other. It is that I might know that sensitivity to You, that willingness to admit my sin, and that openness for cleansing."

It is, after all, a matter of conscience.

CHAPTER SEVEN

Uncommon Love

Then David lamented with this lamentation over Saul and over Jonathan his son, and he told them to teach the children of Judah the Song of the Bow; indeed it is written in the Book of Jasher:

"The beauty of Israel is slain on your high
   places!
How the mighty have fallen!
Tell it not in Gath,
Proclaim it not in the streets of Ashkelon—
Lest the daughters of the Philistines rejoice,
Lest the daughters of the uncircumcised
   triumph.

"O mountains of Gilboa,
Let there be no dew, nor let there be
   rain upon you,
Nor fields of offerings.
For the shield of the mighty is cast away there!
The shield of Saul, not anointed with oil.
From the blood of the slain,
From the fat of the mighty,
The bow of Jonathan did not turn back,
And the sword of Saul did not return empty.

"Saul and Jonathan were beloved and pleasant
   in their lives,

And in their death they were not divided;
They were swifter than eagles,
They were stronger than lions.

"O daughters of Israel, weep over Saul,
Who clothed you in scarlet, with luxury;
Who put ornaments of gold on your apparel.

"How the mighty have fallen in the midst
  of the battle!
Jonathan was slain in your high places.
I am distressed for you, my brother Jonathan;
You have been very pleasant to me;
Your love to me was wonderful,
Surpassing the love of women.

"How the mighty have fallen,
And the weapons of war perished!" (2 Sam.
1:17-27).

David was heartbroken about the news. The Philistines had moved against Israel, and in the fighting King Saul and Jonathan, and all Saul's sons except one, were killed. Israel had suffered a major defeat.

David, having heard this information, sat down and composed a eulogy, which is recorded in the first chapter of 2 Samuel. Here we see David's writing at its best. After Saul was killed, David was called in by the people of Judea and was anointed king.

LI'L ABNER

But Abner, one of Saul's men who had somehow escaped the massacre, found Saul's remaining son, Ishbosheth, and made him king over Israel. That meant a divided kingdom with two kings, one over Judah, and one over Israel. Immediately civil war broke out.

David had had his problems with Saul. Once Saul was out of the way, he might well have thought, *My problems are over*. That rarely happens. Instead, we overcome old problems usually to discover that new challenges are there to take their place. God simply does not sponsor extended vacations. Jesus said, "Come aside…and rest *a while*" (Mark 6:31, italics added). Our goal in this life is not to be overcomers retired. No, we stay in the battle; we remain obedient for the duration.

In this very difficult situation, David behaved himself remarkably well. And in the midst of all the feuding and bloodletting—all the terribly dangerous situations—David demonstrated a remarkable capacity to love.

AN UNCOMMON LOVE

It is upon this love that I want to concentrate. In the eulogy, of course, we have a beautiful statement of his love for Jonathan. It is perfectly predictable. Jonathan was the best friend David ever had. He was deeply grieved at the loss.

Surprising, however, was the statement David made concerning his archenemy Saul. Saul, who had spent much time and energy in his obsessive need to get rid of David, was the one whom David honored in this eulogy. David demonstrated his love for Saul as well.

It is not uncommon in eulogies for many of us to say gracious things about even difficult people. Once they are gone we seem to come up with all kinds of lovely memories, do we not? When we go to a funeral service, we wonder if we are in the wrong room in the funeral parlor! We think to ourselves, *The one they're talking about certainly doesn't fit the description of the person to whom I came to offer last respects!*

But this is certainly not the case as far as David was concerned. While he was inconsistent in some things, he was relentlessly constant in his attitude of honor toward Saul. He had continually spoken well of the king, even during the time Saul was trying to kill him. And although love is not explicitly stated in David's eulogy, the foundations are present here and throughout the rest of his writings.

Is there a secret for developing love for an enemy? What about love for a friend? What is the root of our love for others?

The obvious answer is that all human love must be rooted in our love for the Lord. But how does our love for Christ connect with our love for other people? That is what we want to examine.

Let's look briefly at Psalm 18, which apart from verse 1 is also recorded in 2 Samuel 22 and is directly attributed to King David. We will also look at Psalm 116. While it is not officially attributed to David, it is very similar. In all probability it came from his pen, or was taken from Psalm 18.

Psalm 18:1 starts with a beautiful, simple statement, "I will love You,/O LORD, my strength." That sentence, by the way, was repeated every Sunday in the communion liturgy of the ancient church. The will to love God is crucial to our spiritual lives.

Psalm 116 starts in a similar vein. "I love the LORD, because He has heard/My voice and my supplications."

You may say, "Now, wait a minute. Why, when you are going to talk about loving our enemies and loving our friends, do you quote verses about loving the Lord?"

The answer is this: when David referred to King Saul, he referred to him most often as "the Lord's anointed." And he could have looked at Saul in many other ways. He could have said, "He's obnoxious, he's objectionable, he's crazy, he's dangerous. I detest him, I fear him, I'll have nothing to do with him." But he did not react to him in any of those ways. He saw him one way—as the Lord's anointed. In other words, David did not look at Saul as a human being would see him. He looked upon Saul as God saw him.

THE DIVINE VIEWPOINT

That is the key to loving our enemies. David had learned to look at his enemy not as human beings look at their enemies, but as God looks at them. There is the connection.

But, before we can look at people as God looks at them, we need the *incentive* to do it. We need to have our attitude toward God Himself in correct perspective. Or, to put it more simply, we will only begin to love our enemies when we truly love the Lord. Therein lies our incentive, our motivation.

That is why the whole key to understanding David is to

see he had a heart for God. He loved the Lord *beyond all else.* So, in order for us to get a solid base for loving enemies and even loving friends, let us recognize the necessity for first loving the Lord.

When we talk about loving the Lord, we may run into some problems. We need to define our terms. For when we talk about love, we often think in terms of romantic, sentimental love—or long-stemmed roses. But how do you give long-stemmed roses to God? How do you feel romantic and sentimental about God?

Unfortunately, our thinking concerning love is usually in those romantic categories. When we realize that we ought to love God or that we want to love God, we are not even sure what this love for Him is.

"THE BIBLE SAYS..."

The Lord, speaking to Moses, commanded His people in a statement that has been reiterated through Scripture, "You shall love the LORD your God with all your heart, with all your soul, and with all your might" (Deut. 6:5). These three words, *heart*, *soul*, and *might*, give us the clue to what loving God is all about.

1. The heart

In Old Testament terms, the heart was the center of a person's being, the part that discerned, the part that *knew.* To love the Lord with our hearts, then, means to rightly discern the truth about Him. And David clearly did. Let me refer you, for instance, to Psalm 116:5, "Gracious is the LORD, and righteous;/Yes, our God is merciful." David's love for the Lord can be seen in his allowing the Spirit of the Lord to give him discernment. In the most basic of terms, God had revealed Himself to David.

It is important that we connect the words *truth* and *heart.* For there are all kinds of misconceptions about God that abound in our society. If you get into a conversation about the Lord with people at work tomorrow, I'll guarantee you, you will come up with twenty misconceptions in half a day! What people *don't* know about God would fill a library. What they *do* know wouldn't fill a diary.

The reason, of course, is they have not allowed themselves to be exposed to God's Self-revelation in Scripture. If we allow ourselves to imbibe what the Bible teaches and allow the Spirit of God to impart truth to us, our hearts will begin to discern the truth. And, as we respond to the Father, Son, and Holy Spirit with obedience and worship, that response is loving the Lord with our hearts. The truth about Him is that He is not only gracious, righteous, and full of compassion, but He also loved us enough to reach out to us even when we were His enemies—to the extremity of giving His Son.

See how the psalmist described the Lord's actions on our behalf:

> He sent from above, He took me;
> He drew me out of many waters.
> He delivered me from my strong enemy,
> From those who hated me,
> For they were too strong for me.
> They confronted me in the day of my calamity,
> But the LORD was my support.
> He also brought me out into a broad place;
> He delivered me because He delighted in me
> (Ps. 18:16-19).

Our Lord Jesus came down from heaven and took upon Himself our human nature to take hold of us. He drew us out of our spiritual lostness and deadness, and He rescued us from the things that would ruin our lives. He brought us into the spacious place of His blessing which will find its eternal consummation in heaven itself.

Don't ever be satisfied with a heart that is untaught and, accordingly, unmoved concerning who God really is.

There are times we are bitter against Him, angry with Him, desperately upset—sometimes we are just plain ignorant of Him. This is not loving the Lord. Loving God is based first in rightly discerning the truth about who He is, and then bowing to Him as Lord over all in wholehearted obedience and worship.

2. The soul

The soul is the center of the will, of our volitional desire. Soul-love means rightly desiring the Lord and this is expressed for us in Psalm 116:12: "What shall I render to the Lord/For all His benefits toward me?" With the heart I have *discerned* the truth of God; with the soul I *desire* to please and thank Him. I desire to know Him more thoroughly. I desire to behave correctly toward Him and bring everything I am under servitude to Him.

As the psalmist said in another psalm, "For to You, O Lord, I lift up my soul" (Ps. 86:4). Loving God with the soul, then, means desiring to live righteously before Him and responding adequately to Him.

3. Our might

We love God with our might. Might, of course, speaks of action. We are to love God with everything we have. We *discern* who He is, we *desire* to respond, and then with our might we *do* what is His will. We do everything that He has told us to do. In actual fact, our obedience to His commands is the essence of the demonstration of our love for Him.

"If you love Me," said our Lord, "keep My commandments" (John 14:15). And this statement refers to far more than our initial trust in Christ or the moment of our dedication. The psalmist decided, "I will call upon Him as long as I live" (Ps. 116:2). That is another way of saying, "I will depend upon Him, I will trust Him."

Our love for Christ is summarized best in what the apostle John told us: "We love Him because He first loved us"

(1 John 4:19). And it is amplified in what the apostle Paul told us: "But God demonstrates His own love toward us, in that while we were still sinners, Christ died for us" (Rom. 5:8).

I believe that the final question the Lord is going to ask us when we stand before Him is the same question Christ asked Peter after His resurrection: "Simon, son of Jonah, do you love Me?" (John 21:16). Forget the others for a moment. Put them to one side. Do you really *love* Jesus Christ? If you do, tell Him so. And commit yourself with all your heart, soul, and might!

LOVING THE UNLOVELY

Because David was able to say deep in His heart, "I love the Lord," he also had the capacity and the incentive to love his enemy, Saul. He learned to see Saul not as a man would see him, but as the Lord saw him. We have all met women who have been terribly abused by former husbands. Often, they remain resentful and bitter, which is understandable and even predictable. But remember, if you are in that situation and are simply exhibiting resentment and bitterness to the person who has abused you, you are behaving predictably and understandably because you are looking at the person from a human viewpoint—as any person would.

How does the Lord look at that person who abused you? The Lord looks at that person as a very precious, though fallen, part of creation. He looks at that person as being potentially redeemable, one who can eventually be transformed into the image of Christ. In the one who has misused you, God sees a possible adornment for heaven— someone who could be to the praise of God's glory for all eternity before watching, wondering myriads of angels!

You say, "Come on. We're talking about a bum who beat his wife and destroyed their marriage. This is not some strayed seraph."

The only way we can begin to consider loving our enemies is when we are prepared to think the way David thought. Now that I am cultivating a heart for God, I can commit myself to loving my enemies. I will start by relating to them as God relates to them. And that most certainly is what David did. We never heard him speak of "that crazy king," or "the royal airhead," or "the maniac monarch." Instead, David honored Saul at all costs. Every time he was confronted with Saul, he referred to him as "the Lord's anointed."

The key to loving enemies, then, is to see them as God sees them, not as you or I see them. Now, that's tough! But it came with the territory when you decided you were going to develop a heart for God.

Our Lord Jesus made a powerful statement, recorded in the Book of Matthew: " 'You have heard that it was said, "You shall love your neighbor and hate your enemy." But I say to you, love your enemies,...and pray for those who spitefully use you and persecute you' " (5:43-44).

Incidentally, sometimes in the Sermon on the Mount the Lord talked about what the people had "heard said," and other times what they had "seen written." When He referred to what they had seen written, He meant what was recorded in the Old Testament. What they had heard said referred to the oral tradition that had grown up as interpretations of what was written in the Scriptures. You won't find a Scripture verse that reads, "Love your neighbor and hate your enemy." That was a popular redefinition given by rabbis who presumably did not like their enemies either. But it was never something that God said.

What Jesus said, however, was unequivocal. The statement was, "Love your enemies." And therein lies one of the greatest challenges—equally one of the greatest opportunities—for Christian discipleship imaginable. Who else on earth is going to do *that*?

ENEMY-LOVE

But how, then, do we demonstrate Christian love for an enemy in a practical way? Let me mention several biblical patterns.

1. *Christian love refuses to take advantage of the enemy.*
On two occasions David had a golden opportunity to get rid of Saul. On one occasion, Saul moved into the back of the cave where David and his men were hiding, trying to find the "men's room." While he was using the facility, he was surrounded by David and his men. They could have killed him, and Saul would have never known what happened. David refused.

The other incident was mentioned earlier when a deep sleep fell on Saul and all his bodyguards. David, you will recall, went right down into the center of the camp and literally stood over the sleeping Saul, whose spear was stuck in the ground. David's man said, " 'God has delivered your enemy into your hand this day. Now therefore, please, let me strike him at once with the spear, right to the earth; and I will not have to strike him a second time!' " (1 Sam. 26:8). But David wouldn't let him. Why? Enemy love refuses to take advantage.

David replied, " 'Do not destroy him; for who can stretch out his hand against the LORD's anointed, and be guiltless?' " (1 Sam. 26:9). He understood what was written in Scripture. "Vengeance is Mine, and recompense," the Lord said (Deut. 32:35).

I can refuse to take advantage over my enemies only when I understand that revenge, or "getting even," is not my prerogative. Vengeance belongs to the Lord, and I must leave it with Him. That is hard, but that is how it is.

Recently, I heard of a lady who had been terribly abused by her husband. He eventually had asked her to do something for him. Her response was, "Never, as long as I live, will I do anything that is going to help you." She has set a course for the rest of her life. Unless she cultivates a soft heart through Christ, she will stay totally committed to bitterness and getting even. Oh, it may hurt her husband who hurt her, but eventually it will destroy her, too.

The Christian must have a different approach. He or she is called by God to love an enemy, which among other things means refusing to take the advantage and get even.

2. Love respects the enemy's dignity.

After the enemies of Saul had killed him, the Philistines mutilated his body. They cut off his head in a gesture of disrespect, and then they took the rest of his body to Beth Shan where they nailed it up on the walls so everyone could see the shame of the late majestic king (see 1 Sam. 31:9-10).

The people of Jabesh Gilead, when they heard, were appalled and outraged. At considerable risk to themselves, they took the body down and gave it a proper burial, demonstrating that they had a sense of honor toward their fallen king. When David heard about it, he sent a message to the men of Jabesh Gilead and warmly commended them for their actions. Even though Saul had terribly mistreated him, David respected his enemy's dignity (see 2 Sam. 2:4-6).

3. Godly love genuinely regrets the enemy's downfall.

" 'The beauty of Israel is slain on your high places!/How the mighty have fallen!' " (2 Sam. 1:19). How did David refer to Saul in his eulogy? As "the beauty of Israel," the "mighty" of the Lord of hosts. He deeply and genuinely regretted Saul's downfall.

You know, there is something about human nature. When we have been knocked down by an enemy, we love to see that enemy fall. "At last they got what was coming to them," we say. Enemy love, however, is not about to do that. For love, as 1 Corinthians 13 tells us, does not rejoice in iniquity.

4. Enemy love avoids triumphalism.

" 'Tell it not in Gath,/Proclaim it not in the streets of Ashkelon—/Lest the daughters of the Philistines rejoice,/Lest the daughters of the uncircumcised triumph' " (2 Sam. 1:20). David was saying, "Don't tell the Philistines what happened to Saul. If you do, their daughters will come out with their cymbals, sing their songs, and dance in the streets of Gath and Ashkelon. They will rejoice in the downfall of Saul. Their party will know no bounds! So don't tell them."

David put down a security blackout on the news. Today's TV and newspaper reporters would be greatly upset. "We have the right to know!" they would say. And David's answer? "Well, you sure won't! Because we're not telling you about this."

5. Enemy love recounts the enemy's strength.

" 'From the blood of the slain,/From the fat of the mighty,/The bow of Jonathan did not turn back,/And the sword of Saul did not return empty' " (2 Sam. 1:22). He was saying, "Whatever else you want to think about Saul, he was a superb warrior. When it came to handling the enemies of God, his sword never turned back. And his son Jonathan was just as brave and courageous. His bow never turned back from dealing with the enemies of the circumcised people."

One of the things you do in enemy love is to try very hard to find the enemy's strength and give credit where it is due. That, likewise, does not come easily. Our natural tendency is to maximize our strengths and minimize our weaknesses, while minimizing our enemy's strengths and maximizing his or her weaknesses. Enemy love, hard as it may be, does exactly the reverse.

6. Enemy love restrains criticism.

" 'Saul and Jonathan were beloved and pleasant in their lives,/And in their death they were not divided;/They were swifter than eagles,/They were stronger than lions' " (2 Sam. 1:23).

Quite frankly, Saul and Jonathan had their problems. We know that. David decided at this time not to capitalize on criticism. He decided to draw a veil over the weaknesses, to forgo the criticism. It was simply not necessary.

7. Enemy love reveres the enemy's well-being.

" 'O daughters of Israel, weep over Saul,/Who clothed you in scarlet, with luxury;/Who put ornaments of gold on your apparel' " (2 Sam. 1:24). What was left of Saul? Some charred ashes in an urn. That was all. Oh—and his memory. So what did David ask? He asked the people to remember with gratitude the things that they could remember with gratitude. He was concerned that whatever was left of the enemy might be revered.

And when our Lord teaches, " 'You have heard that it was said, "You shall love your neighbor and hate your enemy." But I say to you, love your enemies...that you may be sons of your Father in heaven' " (Matt. 5:43-45), we have a new way to listen. David, whatever else we may say about him, was a man after God's own heart. And he certainly knew what it was to love the Lord and to love his enemy.

WHO IS YOUR ENEMY?

Let us pause here a moment. Who is that person who has disgraced you or caused you harm? What is your reaction? Are you grasping the opportunity to be uniquely Christian, or are you allowing the consensus of opinion to speak to you and drag you down to similar behavior?

When you sit in the typing pool at the office and they are all talking about how they have been mistreated by management, or abused by spouses, do you go along with the whole thing and talk just as they do? Or do you derive your world view from people who love the Lord and obey His Word?

I beg you—don't miss out on the incredible possibility of loving your enemy. Say no to harboring criticism, maximizing others' faults, and minimizing their strengths. Live Christianly before God and your fellow human beings.

❖

CHAPTER EIGHT

Paraders of the Lost Ark

Again David gathered all the choice men of Israel, thirty thousand. And David arose and went with all the people who were with him from Baale Judah to bring up from there the ark of God, whose name is called by the Name, the LORD of Hosts, who dwells between the cherubim. So they set the ark of God on a new cart, and brought it out of the house of Abinadab, which was on the hill; and Uzzah and Ahio, the sons of Abinadab, drove the new cart. And they brought it out of the house of Abinadab, which was on the hill, accompanying the ark of God; and Ahio went before the ark. Then David and all the house of Israel played music before the LORD on all kinds of instruments made of fir wood, on harps, on stringed instruments, on tambourines, on sistrums, and on cymbals....Then David danced before the LORD with all his might; and David was wearing a linen ephod. So David and all the house of Israel brought up the ark of the LORD with shouting and with the sound of the trumpet. And as the ark of the LORD came into the City of David, Michal, Saul's daughter, looked through a window and saw King David leaping and whirling before the LORD; and she despised him in her heart (2 Sam. 6:1-5,14-16).

Initially, David had ruled only half the nation. After King Saul had been killed, David was anointed king of Israel, but you will remember that Saul's son, Ishbosheth, was anointed king of the other half of the kingdom. So there were at first two kings over a divided kingdom. Later, David became king over the united kingdom.

David immediately decided that Jerusalem should be the royal city of the united kingdom. Previously, the north side of Jerusalem had been overcome by the Benjaminites when they had gone into the land under Joshua. The southern part of the city, which included Mount Zion, was held by the Jebusites, and the people of Israel had never been able to overthrow them.

David approached the matter in a very simple way. He first examined all the methods that had been tried, but had failed, in overthrowing the Jebusites. "Mount Zion is impregnable, even lame and blind people could hold it," the Jebusites boasted (see 2 Sam. 5:6).

But David discovered a basic weakness. The Jebusites had carved a watercourse through solid rock to transport their water supply. While the Jebusites slept one night, David slipped in his army through the watercourse. The Jebusites woke up the next morning to find the Israelites smiling down at them, in charge of their habitation. Thus, King David captured Mount Zion. David united Jerusalem, and Jerusalem became the capital city of a united Israel.

David determined something else. Worship had been sadly neglected in the life of Jerusalem for many years. To rectify the situation, David knew the ark of the Lord must be returned to its proper place in Jerusalem. Thus, we pick up the text in 2 Samuel 6.

The Ark of the Covenant is a central part of the Old Testament story. Always remember, the Old Testament is highly significant because, as someone has said so well, "The New is in the Old concealed; the Old is in the New revealed." The tremendous symbolism of the Old Testament gives us graphic insight into New Testament truths. In fact, much New Testament truth is unintelligible without the help of the Holy Spirit to understand Old Testament stories. And the ark of the Lord is certainly one of these truths to be so understood.

GOD'S PRESENCE

The ark is a symbol of the Divine Presence. Sometimes it is called the Ark of the Covenant, other times it is called the Ark of the Testimony. The reason for this is that in Exodus 25 God gave some construction blueprints to His people with whom He had made a covenant. They were, of course, the people of Israel.

The Israelites had been in bondage in Egypt, but God had chosen to bring them out. In the wilderness, He made a promise to them. In fact, He had earlier made the promise to their forefather Abraham: He would be their God, and they should be His people. After God had delivered them out of Egypt and led them into the wilderness, He reaffirmed this covenant. In fact, He constantly reaffirmed the covenant.

He wanted them to realize that they could always count on His promise. So He gave them something visible to help them remember that the covenant was the basis of their relationship with Him. He told Moses there in the wilderness, as recorded in Exodus 25, that he was to make a tabernacle, and in this tabernacle he was to have an ark. The word *ark* simply means "a chest" or "a box." In fact, when we read that Joseph was placed in a coffin in Egypt (see Gen. 50:26), the word for "coffin" is the same as the one for "ark."

The Ark of the Covenant was approximately four feet long, two feet wide, and two feet high. It was made of acacia wood and covered with gold. The lid was of solid gold, and on the gold lid were carvings of two cherubim that faced each other. Four rings were placed on the sides of the ark, and poles were placed through the rings for use in carrying the ark.

The ark was placed in the Holy of Holies in the tabernacle and hidden by curtains so the people of Israel could never see it. Only the high priest was allowed to enter there, and even he was allowed to enter only one day each year, on the Day of Atonement. Thus, there was in the center of the camp of the Israelites a tabernacle that symbolized the presence of God. And God's presence reminded the people He had made a covenant with them: He was their God, and they were His people.

It was impossible for them to come out of their tents each morning without remembering. Every tent faced toward the central place of the camp, which was the tabernacle. And the part of the tabernacle that was most notable was the Holy of Holies in which the ark, the symbol of God's presence, was to be found. Thus, every morning every Israelite, coming out of his tent, was promptly confronted with a reminder of the covenant: "I am your God; you are My people."

STRIKING A BALANCE

Some people focus on the transcendence of God—He is so high and holy they cannot approach Him. Others stress His immanence—God is their friend, available at all times. The biblical balance is that we keep both in tension. We must never act as if He is remote, but we must never allow Him to degenerate into being our buddy. He is at once transcendent and immanent.

The Ark of the Covenant helps us remember both aspects. The ark was always covered by day by the cloud and by night by the pillar of fire. It gave the Israelites a sense of the transcendence of God—that He is high and holy—and they could not look at Him. Yet at the same time, when they saw the cloud and the pillar of fire, they were wonderfully reminded that He was in their presence.

During the years of Saul's reign, Israel totally lost contact with the Ark of the Covenant. There was no realization of the ark's being central in the life of the nation. It had been under Moses, but it was not under Saul. David, upon getting the kingdom united and establishing the new capital, in so many words said, "The Ark of the Covenant must be restored to its proper place, so people are constantly reminded of God's presence in their midst and that they are God's people."

THE TEN COMMANDMENTS

Most of us are familiar with the Ten Commandments and know that they were written on two tablets of stone. But did you know the Ten Commandments were placed inside the Ark of the Covenant? That is why it is called, in addition to the Ark of the Covenant, the Ark of the Testimony, for the law of God, the Ten Commandments, were called among other things, "the Testimony."

The Ten Commandments are God's testifying about Himself, God's revealing His character. Do you want to know what God is like? Read the Ten Commandments. You will find out what God is for and what He is against. Strangely, this one aspect of the Ten Commandments is almost universally overlooked. The ark is not only a reminder of God's covenant with His people and His presence among them, but it is also a reminder of the nature and character of God. Thus, it is aptly called the Ark of the Testimony.

Why was it such a problem that, during Saul's reign, the people forgot about the ark? Because to forget the ark was to forget God's covenant, His presence, and His holiness of character. When this shortcoming occurs, you have problems in people's hearts and in the nation itself. This situation was precisely what David inherited, and he quickly reestablished the centrality of the ark to correct this deficiency.

ARK OF MERCY

In both the King James and the New King James Versions the lid, or cover, of the ark is called the "mercy seat." It was, literally, the "place of atonement."

I am sure you are familiar with the expression *Yom Kippur*. Yom Kippur is the Hebrew expression meaning the "Day of Atonement." The Day of Atonement was vitally important in the spiritual life of Israel. One day each year the people were told to gather at the tent of meeting. The high priest was to prepare himself meticulously. He was told how to bathe in preparation, what clothing to wear, what animals to take for sacrifice, where to stand, and what to do. As priest, he was to bring the people before God and act on their behalf.

First of all, he was to have ceremonial cleansing for his own sins because he was not perfect. Then he was to cleanse the whole of the tabernacle. Then and only then could he come before God to have cleansing for the sins of all the people. This is Yom Kippur, the Day of Atonement.

The important insight here is this: the high priest went into the Holy of Holies to stand before the Ark of the Covenant, and he brought the blood of the offering and sprinkled it on the lid of the ark, the place of atonement. He offered the blood of an innocent victim shed for the sins of the people. And he prayed to the Lord on behalf of all the people and asked God to forgive them.

Then he went out to where the people were. He selected two goats. One of the goats was slain, and once again the blood was sprinkled on the place of atonement. The other goat (called the scapegoat) had hands laid upon it, and the sins of the people were symbolically placed upon it. Then it was led off into the wilderness.

The Day of Atonement, then, is a marvelous picture of God's forgiving the sins of the people on the basis of the shed blood of an innocent victim. In the Old Testament, it could only be done when God said, where God said, and by whom God said. And the only place atonement could take effect was at the Ark of the Testimony, the Ark of the Covenant, the place of atonement.

David knew all this, but Saul had forgotten it. Priority number one for David was making the ark absolutely central once again in the life of Israel.

Let me, at this point, voice a concern. There is no question that without the presence of the ark, the people began to ignore God. Imagery that expresses the presence of the Lord is vital to our faith and worship.

IMAGE AND REALITY

The symbol will always speak of a reality. The Ark of the Covenant spoke of the covenant God had with His people. Thus, David brought back the symbols of covenant. But the symbol, in and of itself, did not provide an automatic solution to the problem of the people's ignoring the Lord. The response of faith is mandatory. If there is not reality in one's heart, simply carting the ark back onto the center stage of worship, hoping that the symbol by itself will solve the problem, will not do.

I am all in favor of bringing Christian symbolism and imagery back into our worship of the living God. But I am desperately concerned about people who merely want to bring something symbolic into the church and leave God out of it. One of the biggest insults a human being can ever pay God is to say, "Lord, I want all the trappings of Your presence, but I don't want You. I want You to solve my problems, but I don't want a covenant with You."

I don't know if you have ever noticed this phenomenon, but it is relatively common to have people worship their idols from Sunday noon to late Saturday night and then turn toward the ark on Sunday morning for an hour and ten minutes. They don't want God to change them, but they do feel that there is some merit in engaging in the trappings of Christ for an hour a week. In the center of their lives is an idol, but there are religious affiliations as well.

Jill and I had an experience with proper religiosity years ago when an upright family in the city where we lived had a daughter who got pregnant without bothering to get married. This event caused considerable consternation for the family. They were absolutely traumatized by the whole thing. They looked for every way imaginable to get out of the fix, and in the end they thought of us. They knew we were engaged in Christian work with young people.

They called us on the telephone and said, "Would you be prepared to have this young lady stay with you throughout the pregnancy and look after her? She's all mixed up, and we're upset—it's such a mess. And we know you could be helpful to her." Then they said, "But we don't want her converting."

Don't want her *converting*! They had to be kidding!

But they weren't. They wanted to keep the idol of good times right in the middle of her life so that she could continue doing her own thing her own way. But they were very happy for us to bring our ark of service in until the pressure was off. You know, "Just keep Christianity in its proper place." That will never work.

Do you know anybody like that when it comes to the

Lord? They are not against Him. Oh, no, by no stretch of the imagination are they against Him. But they are not for Him, either. They just sort of sidestep the issue of commitment.

THE CYNICS' CORNER

Having said all that, though, there is an attitude that I believe is even worse than such nominalism. Whereas a person may repent of nominalism and become a vital Christian, turning from this other problem is infinitely more difficult. I am talking about cynicism.

While David was involved in reestablishing the centrality of the ark and was caught up in worship, his wife, Michal, Saul's second daughter, was in the palace, peeping around the drapes. As she saw David worshiping and dancing before the Lord, praising God and honoring Him, she "despised" him in her heart. She was cynical about his faith in the ark, and therefore embarrassed by his exuberance.

You will find cynics in every congregation. They are utterly predictable. They are cynical about theology, the preaching of the Word, the organization of the church. They are usually cynical about the leadership of the congregation and sometimes about the people of the church. But worst of all, most cynics eventually become cynical about God Himself.

They choose not to believe that God is a covenant-making God who offers them forgiveness. They do not believe that God's laws are the way to go. And the thing I will never understand is *why they keep on coming!*

I want you to notice that as a result of her cynical attitude, Michal had no children to the day of her death (see 2 Sam. 6:23). She was barren. Let me say this straightforwardly. When it comes to spiritual fruit in your life, healthy productivity will never spring up out of a heart cynical toward the living God and His people. I urge you to put away the very last trace of cynicism from your heart and life.

A NEW COVENANT

In Hebrews 9, we are introduced to a Christian understanding of the application of these truths. We talked earlier about the covenant God made with Moses and about how the Ark of the Covenant was a symbol of His presence among the people. The Bible teaches us that a new covenant has been made and that when we come to the communion table, we hear the words, "This is the blood of the new covenant." When God the Father sent Jesus into the world, He, Christ, became the mediator of the new covenant.

In the old covenant, the high priest had to offer a sacrifice for both his own sins and the sins of the people. Our Lord Jesus Christ comes into the presence of the living God not only as our High Priest but also as the Sacrifice (see Heb. 7-8). He offered Himself without spot to God. His blood was shed for the remission of all our sins. He went down into death and buried our sins there. He rose again from the dead and went into the presence of the living God, where He ever lives to make intercession for us. The Lamb of God has taken away the sins of the whole world.

Not only that, but also we realize there is a new means of atonement. It is the Cross. And as we glory in the Cross, we see Christ dying once and for all for the sins of the whole world. We see now not an ark on which the blood of bulls and goats is sprinkled, but we see the living Lord Jesus having died on the cross for our sins, making us as Paul said, "accepted in the Beloved."

We don't look to the tablets of stone inside the ark. We realize that when we were converted to Christ, the Spirit of the living God came into our hearts. And now we find that the law of God, instead of being written in tablets of stone, has been written, as the Scriptures say, in the fleshly tablets of our hearts (see 2 Cor. 3:3). The heart for God is one which is given over to the fullness of the Holy Spirit as He makes the Word of God alive and real to us

Today we need some Davids who recognize that in all our ecclesiastical activity we have lost the sense of divine centrality. In our church planning sessions we need men and women who will not allow us to move in a sophisticated drift away from the recognition that it is the Lord from whom we come, to whom we go, by whom we survive, and for whom we live.

Preachers preparing messages must remember that, in their quest for relevance and in their search for apt illustrations, it is Christ whose presence they preach. Congregations need constant reminders that arriving late and ill-prepared, hot and bothered from an early morning family feud, may be indicative that the ark is lost from their Sunday worship.

When he returned the ark to Jersusalem and paraded it before the people, David did for his nation more than he could ever imagine. God grant that we might, in our day, be like him—paraders of the lost ark.

CHAPTER NINE

A Heart of Kindness

Now when Mephibosheth the son of Jonathan, the son of Saul, had come to David, he fell on his face and prostrated himself. Then David said, "Mephibosheth?" And he answered, "Here is your servant!" So David said to him, "Do not fear, for I will surely show you kindness for Jonathan your father's sake, and will restore to you all the land of Saul your grandfather; and you shall eat bread at my table continually." Then he bowed himself, and said, "What is your servant, that you should look upon such a dead dog as I?"

And the king called to Ziba, Saul's servant, and said to him, "I have given to your master's son all that belonged to Saul and to all his house. You therefore, and your sons and your servants, shall work the land for him, and you shall bring in the harvest, that your master's son may have food to eat. But Mephibosheth your master's son shall eat bread at my table always." Now Ziba had fifteen sons and twenty servants. Then Ziba said to the king, "According to all that my lord the king has commanded his servant, so will your servant do." "As for Mephibosheth," said the king, "he shall eat at my table like one of the king's sons." Mephibosheth had a young son whose name was Micha. And all who dwelt in the house of Ziba were servants of Mephibosheth. So Mephibosheth dwelt in Jerusalem, for he ate continually at the king's table. And he was lame in both his feet (2 Sam. 9:6-13).

David's kingdom expanded dramatically. He was extremely successful in his various military campaigns and demonstrated remarkable gifts of administration. The kingdom of Israel under him reached its high point.

(Parenthetically, let me suggest you read 2 Samuel 8 with the benefit of both an atlas of the Old Testament and some modern maps. As you put the two geographies together, you will realize the size of the kingdom that David established, which was perpetuated by his son Solomon. This is of particular interest to us today because you will find that much on the six o'clock news every evening seems to deal with the area known as David's kingdom.)

It is significant that while David was overseeing the massive task of establishing this kingdom, he still labored under an intimate, personal concern for those around him. And he did not let go of his loyalty toward the household of his old enemy, Saul, and his dearest friend, Jonathan.

There was a servant from the house of Saul whose name was Ziba. They brought him to David, and the king said to him, "Are you Ziba?" And he said, "At your service!"

Then the king said, "Is there not still someone of the house of Saul, to whom I may show the kindness of God?" And Ziba told him of a son of Jonathan who was lame.

"Where is he?" David asked.

Before long, Mephibosheth, the son of Jonathan, had come to David. He prostrated himself before the king.

David said to him, "Do not fear, for I will surely show you kindness for Jonathan your father's sake, and will restore to you all the land of Saul your grandfather; and you shall eat bread at my table continually."

Then Mephibosheth bowed and said, "What is your servant, that you should look upon such a dead dog as I?"

SHOWING GOD'S KINDNESS

It is a very gentle, tender story told in the midst of all the others we read about David. Notice that the first question David asked was, "Is there a survivor from the house of Saul to whom I can show kindness for Jonathan's sake?" David wanted to be especially kind to any survivors of the house of Saul—for the sake of Jonathan. It was not just a little favor that David wanted to do for those survivors. 2 Samuel 9:3 tells us he wanted to show God's kindness.

Now this is an absolutely fascinating expression in the original text. The Hebrew word translated "kindness" here is a very common Old Testament word. It is translated by a variety of English words in the many editions of the Bible available to us. In the older versions, you will often see it as "lovingkindness," a word we rarely use any longer. A similar rendering in the newer translations is "steadfast love." You will also find it translated "grace," "mercy," or "love." The overall idea has to do with a personal commitment to be loving, kind, merciful, and gracious in an enduring steadfast way, especially from one who is in a position to help another of lesser means.

Because of its repeated usage, this Hebrew word is key to the understanding of the Old Testament. And because it is crucial to the understanding of the Old Testament, it is obviously important in our understanding of the New Testament as well. In dealing with God's kindness, we will need to look at some other scriptural passages.

A MAJOR BIBLICAL THEME

In Exodus 34, we have a very important event explained

to us relative to God's kindness. God, this passage shows, chose to reveal Himself to His people through Moses. This event cannot be overlooked, because the most important thing a human being can do is to know God. Why?

The human race, by creation, is related to three distinct realms: the animal kingdom, the vegetable kingdom, and the mineral kingdom. You can look at these different "kingdoms," these different areas of Creation, and find very close affinities. But there is also a marked difference between humanity and the animal, vegetable, and mineral kingdoms to which we are related.

What is that difference? The Scriptures teach that the fundamental difference is that we, as human beings, have a spiritual dimension, which enables us to know God and to be known by Him. This dimension is what makes humanity unique, and therefore the most important thing that we as human beings can experience is the knowledge of God.

Now, here is the rub. We cannot know God or "figure Him out" merely in terms of our human, rational understanding. To attempt such a thing would be like trying to get ten thousand gallons of water into a thimble. It simply will not fit. The onus, therefore, is on God to reveal Himself to us. That is basically what happened in Exodus 34. In that passage we discover some extremely important truths about the Lord.

1. God's character

There is an ancient statement here concerning God's taking the initiative in revealing Himself in order that He might be known. Notice how He revealed Himself. In Exodus 34:6, He said, "The LORD, the LORD God, merciful and gracious, long-suffering, and abounding in goodness and truth."

God was saying to Moses, and through Moses to the people, "Look, I want you to know Me. And this is what I'm like." He wanted them, and us, to know from the very beginning that His character demonstrates His kindness.

Some people have a problem with this idea. They say, "You're trying to tell me God is good and kind? Listen, I want you to know something. I'm out in the big, cold, cruel world, and it's crummy out there."

Not long ago, a lady came to me and said, "My eighteen-year-old daughter is working in the emergency unit of one of the Chicago hospitals. She's had real Christian faith all her life. But this week she came home and said, 'I can't believe in a God of goodness any longer. There are just too many rotten, nasty, despicable things happening in this world.' "

It is very important for us to recognize the problem that young woman was struggling with. We must understand that many factors go into the working of our world as it is in the present age. We are a fallen humanity. Thus, we have a corrupt society. There is an evil presence in the world. All these powerful factors produce problems in our world.

But! Alongside a fallen humanity, which was caused by the rebellion of *our* race, there is an eternal God who is forever committed to being good and kind. That is His nature. He is kind in spite of our inhumanity to each other. And the evil that we see is directly attributable to our abuse of our God-given freedom. For God to stop all our evil acts would be to invade the very area in which He has given human beings freedom and responsibility. But while He allows us our freedom, and all the various consequences of that freedom, He works in the midst of our sin to show us continually His goodness and kindness.

The Scriptures are a chronicle, in this sense, of how He brings good out of evil and blessing out of cursing. He brings redemption out of our rebellion, eternal restoration out of our material abuse, and divine healing out of our human aberration. Therein lies the majesty of His kindness and His goodness.

2. God's covenant

In addition to His kindness, let us look at His covenant. Deuteronomy 7 is another basic Old Testament passage in which God reiterated what He was doing with the people of Israel. He was their *covenant* God.

God chose Abraham so that through him He might develop a special people. God did not—and does not—want to deal only with individuals. He wanted a society, a nation, with which to deal. He chose Abraham and the people who would come through Abraham to belong to Him and to have a land in which to live out His commands before the rest of the world.

He allowed them to go down into Egypt first to save them from starvation and then to be strengthened through adversity. Then He chose to bring them out of Egypt through a remarkable exodus under Moses' leadership. When they got as far as the wilderness, they began to grumble and murmur against God and His appointed leader. But He chose to stick with them.

When the time came for them to go into the promised land, it was inhabited by fierce, warlike tribes. God chose to intervene in their affairs again and drive out the enemies. All this choosing and intervening, all this initiative taking on the part of God, was attributable to the fact that He had in His kindness made a covenant with His people.

In Deuteronomy 7:12, we read that God promised to keep "the covenant and the mercy" that He had made with the people's ancestors. Again we have that same Hebrew term, translated here as "mercy." Why did He choose Abraham, and why did He give him Isaac, and through Isaac, a whole people? Because He wanted to show the world the kindness of a loving God toward His people. Why did He purify them through discipline in

Egypt? Because He is kind (when the Lord loves, He chastens). Why did He bring them out and put up with their grumblings in the wilderness? Because He is kind. Why did He take the initiative and drive out their foes before them in the promised land? Because He is kind. Why, when they abused His kindness, did He continue being kind down through their history? Because His kindness endures forever!

Stop and look at your life for a moment. Do you see any similarity in pattern? One of the greatest arguments for God's presence in your life is that He allows you to be tried and tested. What He desires is that you and I pass the test! So to understand God's kindness, we must look first at His character, then at His covenant. And we see portrayed in both His kindness, mercy, and steadfast love.

3. God's consistency

Third, if we are to understand kindness, we must look at the consistency of God. Psalm 136 is, at face value, one of the most boring passages you will ever read in your whole life. On the other hand, once you see its purpose it is one of the most exciting pieces of news you will ever hear. It is boring because, of its twenty-six verses, half of them are exactly the same. It was a psalm used in worship by God's people.

It is in the form of a *litany*. The priest would recite the first part of a verse, and the people would respond with the second. The priest, for example, would say, "Oh, give thanks to the Lord, for He is good!" And the people would say, "For His mercy [kindness] endures forever." Then the priest would say, "Oh, give thanks to the God of gods!" And the people would reply again, "For His mercy endures forever." After a time, everyone would understand the point that God is kind and merciful. Twenty-six times!

Now, that might seem monotonous at first. But you have to bear something in mind. When people come to worship, they rarely prepare. They come bustling in from being preoccupied with any number of things and try to collect all their uncollected thoughts. And they say, "Now, what is going on here?...let's see—did I get the roast in the oven?—I forgot it, never mind, it doesn't matter."

One of the great advantages of a litany like Psalm 136 is that—it is marvelous for unprepared worshipers. You don't have to think up anything. You can turn your attention on the Lord Himself. *Anybody* can say, "His mercy endures forever." Even if you are not prepared, by the time you have heard it five times, you get the idea. And if you do it twenty-six times, in the end you might get the message. So don't knock Psalm 136. Its place is in congregational worship.

Do not miss the point of Psalm 136. As the leader of worship rehearses the wonder of God's character, His Creation, and His intervention in the affairs of His people, there is only one proper response. And that is, "He is so kind. He is so good. He is so merciful."

Then notice the last part of that phrase. His kindness and goodness and love are forever enduring. *Forever enduring!*

Over and over and over again, in all kinds of experiences, God has shown Himself to be relentlessly kind. We can touch any area of His character, of His activity, and of His Self-revelation, and we can see shining through it His kindness, His goodness, and His love.

4. *God's compassion*

If we are to understand God's kindness, then, finally, we must look at His compassion. Genesis 32 is our test, and one of my favorite stories. Jacob was having a lonely soliloquy. It was his dark night of the soul. He was in a desolate area, and he had to confront somebody the next morning he did not want to meet. He was going to experience some difficulty, in all probability.

Now, when you find a man on his own, on a dark night,

in a desolate place, about to confront somebody he does not want to meet beause he knows he is going to have trouble, there is a remarkable possibility he will become *very* religious. It has been known to happen in foxholes all over the world, it has happened to you and me, and it was happening to Jacob there.

What did he say as he sat by the River Jordan? "The last time I crossed this Jordan, I had only a staff in my hand. That was all I had to my name. I've been away a long time, and now I'm coming back. I am loaded with possessions. I've got so many cattle, sheep, servants, wives, and kids, I don't deserve any of it."

But wait. This testimony is probably the finest Jacob ever offered. Of all the slimy, slippery characters you ever met, he was the most slippery. He had defrauded his brother; he had developed social chicanery to a fine art. He was superb at being despicable.

Nevertheless, having been a con man for years, he returned to the land in great shape. Now, at last, he said, "And God, I am unworthy of all Your love, Your kindness, Your mercy. I'm unworthy of all You've done for me. God, I don't understand what You could see in me."

Jacob was coming to the point of agreeing with God. He realized that the only reason God is gracious and kind and loving toward us is that He is gracious and kind and loving.

It is not in *us*; it is in *Him!*

The problem is getting people to believe that truth, because we have been encouraged all our lives to believe the world revolves around us. We are the center and circumference of all things, and God somehow revolves around us out there on the periphery.

The man or woman after God's heart corrects that perspective and sees God as the center of his or her world. Only by His kindness do we receive His gifts of love and grace. And there is nothing in us that would merit His kindness.

Jacob, on that dark and lonely night, was beginning to learn about God's compassion.

TO ILLUSTRATE GOD'S KINDNESS

Let us return to 2 Samuel 9, the theme for this chapter. It records a moving illustration of God's kindness, as demonstrated in David's action toward Mephibosheth. I believe he wanted to show God's kindness to Mephibosheth because he had been caught up with it himself.

In his most famous psalm, Psalm 23, David wrote, "Surely goodness and mercy shall follow me/All the days of my life;/And I will dwell in the house of the LORD forever."

When you look at David's life, he was either on the mountain tops or down in the depths of the valleys. Everything was going his way, or nothing was going his way. He was either being swamped by adulation, or he was being terrorized by troublemakers. Yet he could say, "All the days of my life, the good days and the bad days, the high days and the low days, the bright days and the gloomy days, the mountain top days and the deep valley days, all the days of my life I'm sure of something—God's mercy, grace, and kindness. I change; He changes not. Circumstances change; He changes not. Situations change; He changes not."

There were other factors, too. David appreciated Jonathan's love. More than once, Jonathan risked his personal safety for David.

Furthermore, on an earlier occasion when David saved Saul's life, Saul had the audacity to ask David for a promise. "Promise that you will never cut off my name. That you will always allow my descendants to survive," Saul asked. As far as we can see, there was only one descendant left—Mephibosheth. David remembered the promise he made to Saul, for he swore to him under an oath. It was on the basis of a commitment that David showed kindness.

We live in an age, I believe, when we have forgotten that one of the ways we show kindness is by sticking to what we have said. When we make a promise, we must not abuse somebody else's trust. This was all part of David's follow-through. And it is an illustration of God's kindness to us as well.

David's kindness is seen in the aid he offered this gentleman with the unpronounceable name. For Mephibosheth had a terrible disability. When word came that Saul and Jonathan had been killed, there was general panic in the whole area. One of the nurses picked up this little boy, ran for cover, tripped, and dropped him. He was crippled for the rest of his life.

It was rather obvious that he had stayed in hiding during the years that David had been reigning. He probably did not want to be identified as the only survivor of the house of Saul. Perhaps he thought his days would be numbered. Eventually he was called into David's palace, and the first thing King David said to him was, "Don't be afraid." Why? Most likely because Mephibosheth was afraid he would be killed.

But David chose to intervene with kindness in Mephibosheth's affairs, and he touched the lame man's life. It was not because of anything in Mephibosheth, or because David would derive benefit from helping him. Not at all. It was in the heart of David to pass on God's kindness. Oh, that the same might be said of us!

What did David do? "Bring him here," the king commanded. And David gave him all the land of his grandfather Saul! "Let him sit at my table. Give him the position of one of my own sons. For the rest of his days he will be cared for in my household."

There would be an abundance of resources for Mephibosheth because of the kindhearted nature of the king.

A KINDNESS UNDESERVED

In Paul's letter to Titus, the apostle wrote,

For we ourselves were also once foolish, disobedient, deceived, serving various lusts and pleasures, living in malice and envy, hateful and hating one another. But when the kindness and the love of God our Savior toward man appeared, not by works of righteousness which we have done, but according to His mercy He saved us, through the washing of regeneration and renewing of the Holy Spirit, whom He poured out on us abundantly through Jesus Christ our Savior, that having been justified by His grace we should become heirs according to the hope of eternal life (Titus 3:3-7).

Paul picked up the same theme of kindness. None of us are very pleasant people. We are crippled in our personalities, hopeless when it comes to standing before the court of God. But God, even though He sees us in that state, extends mercy toward us, reaches out to us in kindness, takes the initiative, and gives us love we do not deserve. This, my friend, is the thrust of the Christian gospel and it needs to touch our hearts continually.

Do you want to see God's kindness? Look at the cross and see Christ hanging there, assuming our guilt and accepting the holy wrath of a righteous God against our sins. See Him raising up Christ from the dead and telling us that we can know Him in the power of His resurrection. Receive the gift of the Holy Spirit, whom He prepared to shed forth love abundantly into our hearts.

We look at these things, and our hearts are touched. We realize that the whole reason God is dealing with us in this way in Christ is that He has *perpetuated* that covenant He gave to Abraham and to David. He has passed it on through His Son, and today we live in the good of it. In kindness, Jesus says, "Come to Me, all you who labor and are heavy laden, and I will give you rest. Take My yoke upon you and learn from Me, for I am gentle and lowly in heart, and you will find rest for your souls" (Matt. 11:28-29). And He continues to give us His rest.

God is looking for people who will allow themselves to be touched by His grace and mercy and lovingkindness. He is seeking people with a deep desire not only to *know* of His kindness, but also to *show* His kindness through their own lives.

Once again, David is our model. I believe those of us who have been genuinely touched by the kindness of God have a concern for the spiritually needy. Those of us who have been touched by the kindness and grace of God have a concern for the Mephibosheths of the world. It is unthinkable that the grace and mercy of God that led me to repentance would produce no concern for those who need Him most.

Just as God's kindness was mediated through David to Mephibosheth, so God's kindness can be mediated through us to persons around us. In the power of the Holy Spirit we take of the things with which God has blessed us, and we share them with others. We are to be kind, gracious, and generous because of the grace of God.

KINDNESS AND COVENANT

And one last thing. The kindness of God is inextricably connected with a covenant.

Twenty-five years ago I made a covenant of marriage with my wife. I committed my life in marriage to Jill because I loved her. We have maintained that covenant of faithfulness for a quarter century, and I would like to think that I may have another twenty-five years to go. There is a synergism of relationship here: I made the covenant because I loved her, but I love her because I made a covenant. I am not terribly interested in understanding how all this works or in unraveling one factor from the other. I am just happy to have the two forces of love and covenant inexplicably bound up.

If you love and make a covenant, if you are kind and make a promise, that commitment gloriously binds you to go on exhibiting kindness. Perhaps the most unkind thing we can do is to back out on a covenant or put it on hold. In Christ we simply cannot shrug our shoulders and walk away from a promise. He never does that to us.

There is every opportunity in the world to appreciate God's kindness daily and to demonstrate it. Look around you. Seek out individuals who are spiritually crippled. Develop a heart for God that is directed toward those who are materially and physically disadvantaged. Demonstrate God's kindness to those to whom you have made a covenant—your spouse, your brothers and sisters in Christ, your pastor. Remember, in maintaining that covenant, we are doing the kindest possible thing.

The only reason we are here is because of the kindness of God.

CHAPTER TEN

The Repentant Heart

Then the LORD sent Nathan to David. And he came to him, and said to him: "There were two men in one city, one rich and the other poor. The rich man had exceedingly many flocks and herds. But the poor man had nothing, except one little ewe lamb which he had bought and nourished; and it grew up together with him and with his children. It ate of his own food and drank from his own cup and lay in his bosom; and it was like a daughter to him. And a traveler came to the rich man, who refused to take from his own flock and from his own herd to prepare one for the wayfaring man who had come to him; but he took the poor man's lamb and prepared it for the man who had come to him." Then David's anger was greatly aroused against the man, and he said to Nathan, "As the LORD lives, the man who has done this shall surely die! And he shall restore fourfold for the lamb, because he did this thing and because he had no pity."

Then Nathan said to David, "You are the man!"...Then David said to Nathan, "I have sinned against the LORD." And Nathan said to David, "The LORD also has put away your sin; you shall not die" (2 Sam. 12:1-7,13).

No account of the life of King David, and no treatise on having a heart for God, would be complete without particular reference to the events surrounding David's illicit relationship with Bathsheba, the wife of Uriah the Hittite. Approximately twelve months elapsed between the adulterous event and the day that Nathan the prophet confronted David. Psalm 51, of course, is closely related to this particular incident.

David's reaction to his sin of adultery and murder differed little from the response of similarly guilty parties in our day and time: they repent, or they cover it up. In David's case, he did the latter for a year.

You remember the story: David engaged in illicit sexual relations with Bathsheba while her husband was away at war. She became pregnant. To hide what he had done, David made arrangements to bring Bathsheba's husband home. David's hope was that Uriah would make love to his wife, and everyone would assume that the expected baby would be the result of that union. Thus, there would be no questions asked.

But Uriah would not go home. He felt he had a moral responsibility to his men who were out in the field. Why should he enjoy the affections of his wife when his real place was on the front with his men? David, desperate to get him to go home, finally got him drunk. But Uriah still would not go.

Uriah drunk was a better man than David sober.

David, beginning to panic, decided he must get rid of Uriah the Hittite. He sent him back to the front lines with specific instructions to his commanding officer that he was to be put in the heat of the battle and his help and support were to be withdrawn. David wanted him dead, which is exactly what happened. Uriah was killed in battle.

Then, David felt free to marry Bathsheba. Months later, the baby was born with all the external trappings of legitimacy. David continued wearing his royal robes and going about his majestic business. He had his new wife and baby, and he never acknowledged that anything was amiss. Everything was absolutely marvelous on the surface. There was only one thing wrong: his sin had never been addressed.

There is a great tendency in all of us to camouflage what we have done. But if we have a heart for God, what we cover up is like an internal, physical infection. It grows and grows. We may appear relatively healthy on the outside, but if the internal infection is there, eventually it is going to show. And it is going to affect us in a terrible way.

If we do not deal with the things that are fundamentally wrong in our relationship with God, we will ultimately be exposed. We may be able to cover them for a while and continue to go through the motions of being godly. People may feel that everything is all right, and we may even start thinking so, too. But unless something is done about our problems, our unconfessed sins will find us out. They will bring about real spiritual and emotional and physical damage to us and to those whose lives we touch.

God insists that we deal with these things we cover up so that we might be refreshed and restored to communion with Him. For this to happen, confrontation is necessary. It is about such confrontation that I want to address myself. We will look first at Nathan the prophet's confrontation with David. Next we will consider David's confrontation with himself. And then we will examine David's confrontation with God Himself.

THE ROLE OF THE PROPHET

When we speak in terms of confrontation so that spiritual issues might be settled, we have to be sure we have the right kind of person in charge. God sent Nathan the prophet who had a long relationship with David. He was a tested and proven man.

Because we don't like to face the wrongs we have done, very often we react violently if just anybody confronts us with them. And because people who feel they ought to confront know they will probably get a violent reaction, they are less than enthusiastic about doing it. Therefore, what often happens in our churches is that issues of sin are not dealt with at all, and our spiritual lives suffer as a result. We have churches where godliness is preached but not practiced.

Galatians 6:1 tells us clearly, "Brethren, if a man is overtaken in any trespass, you who are spiritual restore such a one in a spirit of gentleness, considering yourself lest you also be tempted." If anybody is caught up in a sin, those members of the church who are spiritual are to talk with the offender that the individual might repent, be salvaged, and return to a position of spiritual well-being. But notice that the emphasis is on those "who are spiritual." Why would they be especially mentioned?

Some people *love* confrontations. They are confrontational in nature. There is nothing they like better than an argument. They take on all comers and are intimidated by none. These people should not be involved in confrontations in the church. People who deal with sin and ungodliness must have a tremendous sense of the spiritual issues involved and must be genuinely humble before the Lord. For as Galatians 6:1 tells us, if we confront somebody about what is wrong in his or her life, we have to be conscious of the fact that we are equally susceptible to the same evil ourselves.

We must confront with great humility and care. It is relatively easy to go to a wounded person and devastate him or her, sometimes to a point beyond recovery. That is not spiritual confrontation, for the whole point of the act is to resolve the sin and recover the soul. It requires somebody who is deeply concerned about both the things of God and the sanctity of the offender.

THE WISDOM OF NATHAN

Nathan went about the task in a most effective way. He went to David and said in essence, "Let me tell you a story." Of course, people love stories, and David was no exception. David relaxed with his friend Nathan in response to a question—"Did you hear the story about the man who only had one ewe lamb?"

"No, tell it to me."

Nathan told the story. The lamb belonged to a poor man as a household pet. But one day a rich man, who already had sheep of his own, grabbed it and cooked it that night for dinner.

David, with righteous indignation because of the gross injustice of the situation, boiled with anger. "The man who did this will die, and will repay four times!" An interesting remark in itself when one considers the difficulty in making repayment if one is dead! But David didn't seem to worry too much about logic. He was very upset about the story.

What a marvelous job Nathan had done. He had set the stage and outlined the problem; he even had David agreeing with him about its being fundamentally wrong before he applied the parable. And then with tremendous candor, Nathan confronted him, saying, "David, *you* are that man."

When we confront people, we have to touch that tender spot deep down in their hearts where they know how good God has been to them in the past. We must remind them of the goodness and the grace of God. Thus, God said to David, "I anointed you king over Israel, and I delivered you from the hand of Saul. I gave you your master's house and your master's wives into your keeping, and gave you the house of Israel and Judah. And if that had been too little, I also would have given you much more!" (2 Sam. 12:7-8).

But we cannot stop at that level alone. It is necessary to confront them about the reality of sin's significance.

Nathan, for example, could have gone to David and said, "Now, David, the Bible says you shall not commit adultery. And you did. Right?"

"Right."

"And the Bible says you shalt not kill, and you did."

"Right."

"And the Bible says thou shalt not bear false witness, and you did. Right?"

And David could have hung his head and said, "I shouldn't—I won't do that again."

But this was not what Nathan did. Instead, he went far deeper. He wanted David to understand the horrible consequence and significance of his sin.

THE POWER OF SIN

We very often isolate only the individual acts themselves that we call *sins*—adultery, killing, lying, or not honoring parents. The deeper problem is not merely the acts but also the power of sin behind them. There are three little phrases here I want you to notice. In 2 Samuel 12:9 Nathan said to David, "Why have you despised the commandment of the Lord, to do evil in His sight?" In verse 10 the Lord said to David, "You have despised Me." And in verse 14 He said, "However, because by this deed you have given great occasion to the enemies of the LORD to blaspheme...."

Not just our sinful acts are bad, not just what we do to people is bad. There is an underlying principle of sin that we need to confront. Listen, when we sin, we despise the Word of the Lord because, knowing what God says, we choose to do what we want. It is out-and-out rebellion. Having despised God's Word leads us to despise God Himself. What we are really saying is, "I'm going to do my own thing because I prefer me to God." And that is an insult to Him. Adultery, lying, and stealing are bad enough. But at the root of those acts we show utter contempt for the God who gave the commands. Well has someone said, "Secret sin on earth is open scandal in heaven."

And if that were not serious enough, we also give a golden opportunity to the enemies of God to be confirmed in their worst suspicions. They believe we are a bunch of hypocrites anyway, and when they see our sin, they say, "There you are! What did we tell you!" The name of Christ is blasphemed, the church of God is dishonored, and the purposes of God are thwarted. All because of our willful fling with evil. When we sin, therefore, far more is involved than an act of adultery, or stealing, or lying. When we sin, we are hating God's Word, despising the Godhead, and giving carte blanche to God's enemies to alibi their own behavior.

Thus, it is clear why confrontation is absolutely necessary so that people might be reminded of the greatness of God's grace and faced with the awesomeness of their sin. Never allow yourself to feel you are going to get away with your sin and that everything will work out.

It won't.

PERSONAL REPENTANCE

Having been confronted by Nathan, David needed to confront himself and deal with his problem. In short, he needed to readjust his heart with God. David finally said to Nathan, "I have sinned against the Lord" (2 Sam. 12:13).

But we must also turn to Psalm 51. There we have the personal confession David wrote after Nathan confronted him over his adultery with Bathsheba. In that psalm, we see David really confronting himself with the reality of his sin. The way he went about his confession—with razor sharp clarity and candor—is especially important for us to see. For in David's repentance, we most certainly have a model for our own.

He began the confession in verse 5, "Behold, I was brought forth in iniquity,/And in sin my mother conceived me."

David was saying, "The reason I acted as I did is that I have an inbuilt propensity to sin. I have a terrible capability for going wrong. Because of ancestral sin, there is something about *me* that is fundamentally awry."

Understanding that reality is basic to a person's confronting himself or herself. In our world it is relatively easy for us to forget the fallenness of our race. It is convenient for us instead to assume we are like everybody else, fairly normal...we have our strong points, and our weak points. But overall, we are pretty nice persons. And sure, we are not perfect. But when all is said and done, who is?

Do you get a feeling of how it is that we slide away from confronting what we really are? God says, by contrast, that there is fundamental propensity to sin within us. And if we are going to be transformed in Christ, we have to confront it and deal with ourselves. Like David did in Psalm 51.

Notice the words he used in verses 1, 2, and 4: *transgressions, iniquity, sin,* and *evil.* Let us briefly touch on those four words.

1. Evil

What is evil? The Bible usually puts it in juxtaposition with good. Evil is the opposite of good. Scripture tells us

God is good. Evil is that which is in opposition to God.

A scientist was standing on a railroad platform, waiting for a friend to arrive. While he waited, an express train passed through the station, and he noticed a man walking along the corridor of the train. Since he was a scientist, his mind began working.

He thought to himself, *How fast is that man traveling? I would imagine he was walking at about 5 miles an hour. But he passed me in a train traveling at 70. But he can't walk at 70 miles an hour. So was he walking at 5 miles an hour, or 70, or perhaps 75 miles an hour? Or 76.333?* That is how insight into the theory of relativity was born! Relative to a person sitting in a seat on the train, he was traveling at 5 miles an hour. Relative to the man standing on the railroad platform, he was traveling at 5 miles an hour related to the speed of the train. In other words, what he was doing depended on what it was related to, which is all terribly confusing.

It is worse for us because we have taken this idea of relativity and pushed it into every part of our thinking. Now a moral issue arises, and we say, "Well, it might be right for you, but it's wrong for me." Or more often we say, "Well, you may think it's wrong, but it's right for me."

My friend, here is where Holy Scripture absolutely "derelativizes" our modern generation. For when we read about evil in this passage, we see exactly what it means. The offender says, "I have done what is evil *in Your sight.*" Not evil relative to another person or to society, not evil relative to what the United States Constitution says, not evil relative to the customs of the day or to what the academics are saying. (Besides, the academics say one thing, the politicians another, the government another, and the people who live in the suburbs something else.)

God says, "You relate what you think to Me. I will tell you what is right and what is wrong. I will tell you what is good, and what is evil."

Thus, David confronted himself. He admitted without hesitation a sinful propensity, a bias, a bent to sin. He had done evil. "And when I say evil," David continued, "I mean that which is fundamentally wrong to God."

The fact that everybody is doing it is irrelevant. If my neighbor claims it is "helpful to me," that is beside the point. The fact it may bring enjoyment has nothing to do with anything. God said it is wrong; therefore, it is evil.

If we are going to confront ourselves, we have to come to terms with the fact that we have this bent to sin, this capability of evil in God's sight.

2. Transgression

The Hebrew word in Psalm 51 means literally "rebellion," or "revolt." Once I know what God says, there is always that possibility I will rebel against it and say, "Well, God, maybe that's what You say. But I want You to know something. I'm not going to do it." That is rebellion, and David had done that. He purposely stepped across the line of light and righteousness.

3. Iniquity

The Hebrew word translated "iniquity" means literally "to twist it." I know what God says, but I am going to alter the meaning and shape it into what I want it to be. Or, I know what God wants, but I am going to twist and pervert His will to fit neatly into what I have decided. David had been guilty of iniquity.

4. Sin

The Hebrew word translated "sin" is related to a word that described some remarkable left-handed men who were experts at slinging stones. They could sling at a hair and never miss. *Sin* means literally "to miss the target." David admitted to sin. In our day, his prayer might have been, "I've gone off track. I've missed my way. I've rebelled against what God said. I've relativized all that people say that God says. And I have perverted and twisted

His Word and finished up with an utterly wicked life-style."

He confronted himself. In Psalm 51:3 he said, "For I acknowledge my transgressions,/And my sin is ever before me." What a terrible thing to have to say.

Remember—probably twelve months had passed since the act was perpetrated. And for twelve months, all outward appearances had been normal. All his other performances had been acceptable. But never a day had gone by without his being confronted in his heart with the immensity of what he had done. His guilt never left him, never escaped him.

Notice the tremendous sense of perspective that was born in his heart as well: "Against You, You only, have I sinned" (v. 4). When we begin to understand that good and evil are measured in terms of who God is and what God says, then we understand that what we have done, *we have done to God*. So it isn't just, "Well I'm not perfect." Or, "You don't expect me to be an angel, do you?" It is a case of, "Lord, I realize that when I pull this thing into perspective, it's against You that I have sinned. And my sense of guilt is perfectly deserved. You are absolutely right in judging me. You are utterly justified in calling me what I am. I have sinned against You."

Here was a man coming to grips with himself. Here was a man getting a touch of reality after twelve months of spiritual insanity.

A CONFRONTATION WITH GOD

David confronted God with a deep sense of contrition and unworthiness. Look what he asked for. "Have mercy upon me, O God,/According to Your lovingkindness;/According to the multitude of Your tender mercies,/Blot out my transgressions" (Ps. 51:1).

Come pleading for mercy. Don't ever dare to ask God for justice. Don't ever come to Him demanding your rights.

Why? Because you will get them! And you will wish you hadn't. Come to Him on the basis of His mercy and appeal to His grace, His unfailing love, and His compassion. Declare your unworthiness, and in deep contrition, ask for forgiveness. That is the way back.

Second, come with frankness concerning your sin. David specified what he had done in Psalm 51:3-4: "For I acknowledge my transgressions,/And my sin is ever before me./Against You, You only, have I sinned,/And done this evil in Your sight."

I remember a friend of mine in England who said something to me a long time ago. "Baby repentance is *sorry* for what it has done. Adult repentance is *regretful* for what it is." If I am merely sorry for what I have done, do you know what I will do? I will go out and do it again. I will come back to confess, "I did it again, Lord. I'm sorry, Lord." That is not mature confession. Mature confession is a deep sense of contrition about what I have done and regret for what I am.

But look! David came with a deep sense of confidence too. For he knew something. He knew that God is always prepared to receive persons who are of contrite heart and who confess their sins. His confidence was not in himself, but in the Lord who promised him forgiveness. "Cleanse me," he said. "Forgive me." Then, "Restore me." And note, "Put me again in a position where I'll teach people Your ways. I believe that people are going to be converted because of this. Look at Jerusalem, and do good there, God."

Suddenly the whole of his mind was clicking back into gear again. He was excited and confident; his soul was restored; he was positive again. Why? Because he was utterly confident in the promises of God.

Do you know what God has promised? He will abundantly pardon. He will remove our sins as far as the east is from the west. He will bury them in the depths of the sea.

He promises to the truly repentant, "Their sins and their lawless deeds I will remember no more" (Heb. 10:17).

Some people who claim to be Christians seem to love spiritual depression and even failure—they are content to have problems. They do not want to be different. They do not want to worship God. They want to hear a speaker now and then and remain a mess. Not so with the man or woman who desires to confront God. That one cries from the depths of the heart, "Cleanse me. Cleanse me."

There is here a godly concern to be restored. "Make me to hear joy and gladness,/That the bones which You have broken may rejoice" (Ps. 51:8). David was about fifty years old. He had many years of experience with the Lord. And he looked at himself and said, "What a disaster I am."

Some people would say, "Well, I guess my days of victory have gone. I'll just have to settle for being a dry, withered caricature of what I'm supposed to be." Not David. He said "Restore me, Lord. Cleanse me, Lord."

Not only that, he asked for a new attitude: "Create in me a clean heart, O God,/And renew a steadfast spirit within me" (Ps. 51:10). Perhaps David recalled here what happened to King Saul, his predecessor. God took His Spirit from him. David said, "Do not cast me away from Your presence,/And do not take Your Holy Spirit from me" (Ps. 51:11).

David was back where he belonged. He had a reactivated heart for God.

Let me ask you a question, point-blank. Is there sin in your life? As you read these pages, is the Holy Spirit pointing out to you wrong and rebellious choices you have made, or a satisfaction with spiritual mediocrity? Can you say to God, "I need Your power, I need Your joy, I need Your cleansing"?

Perhaps you need the assurance that you can still be used

by Him. It may be you sense that He still has something for you to do. I plead with you to confess your sin and ask Him again to move in your life. Will you do it now?

CHAPTER ELEVEN

To Lead and To Follow

Now these are the last words of David.

Thus says David the son of Jesse;
Thus says the man raised up on high,
The anointed of the God of Jacob,
And the sweet psalmist of Israel:

"The Spirit of the Lord spoke by me,
And His word was on my tongue.
The God of Israel said,
The Rock of Israel spoke to me:
'He who rules over men must be just,
Ruling in the fear of God.
And he shall be like the light of the morning
   when the sun rises,
A morning without clouds,
Like the tender grass springing out of the earth,
By clear shining after rain' " (2 Sam. 23:1-4).

S ome time ago *Time* magazine, in dealing with crisis in leadership, noted that when we had only thirteen colonies we seemed to have a remarkable ability to produce superb leadership from a relatively small population. But now, the article continued, we have fifty states, a much larger population, and we don't seem to have the leadership.

As the article was examining various reasons for this phenomenon, a most interesting suggestion was posted. Perhaps the problem was not so much a crisis of leadership as a crisis of "followship."

Have we produced people who are so independently minded, the author asked, that they refuse to follow anybody anywhere at all?

Sobering thought, is it not? While many people say they want effective direction in their lives, they want a direction *they* are prepared to go in, security on their own terms. In order for leadership to work correctly in the Christian church, both the leaders and the followers must have submissive hearts toward God. Let us look in this chapter at the life of David in terms of his heart to lead his people.

From the Scriptures, we can see that David is not only a model of political leadership, but also quite legitimately his life is an illustration of the lordship of Christ in people's lives—how Christ reigns over His people. Leadership and Christ's lordship are not unrelated.

David said that adequate leadership must be in righteousness and in the fear of God. If we are to know righteousness and godly fear, then we must know the lordship of Christ in our lives.

THE MATTER OF AUTHORITY

When we think in terms of leadership, we have to think in terms of authority. The Scriptures clearly teach us that God is the ultimate authority. Without His authority, we would not even exist. Nor could we survive, if His authority could be somehow removed.

But God makes it clear in Scripture that He *delegates* His authority. Romans 13 is the passage that describes how God has delegated His authority to men and women in society so that there might be order through governing authority. Civil authority, then, is absolutely necessary. The alternative is anarchy—no leadership at all. We need leaders who exercise authority so that our society will function with justice and direction. In fact, poor civil authority is usually better than no authority at all.

Scripture, however, is even more specific, for it discusses the necessity of leadership in other areas, such as the family and the church of Jesus Christ. Paul, in 1 Timothy 3, for example, wrote about the qualification of bishops (or overseers) in the church. He said if anyone was going to be a bishop, he must rule his own house properly. Then Paul pointed out a rather obvious thing: if one cannot rule his own family, how on earth can he give leadership in the church of God?

Authority and leadership are needed in the family so we might teach our young people obedience and maintain order in society. If the church of Jesus Christ is to have any sense of godly direction, everybody cannot follow discrete pathways. As a body of believers, we must have objectives, and we must move cohesively together in one direction. That requires authoritative leadership.

A REPERTOIRE OF EXPERIENCE

David learned to lead in God's schoolroom of experience—the same way you and I learn. For instance, in 1 Samuel 22 we read of an early lesson he learned when he was in exile in the cave of Adullam. When his brothers and his father's household heard of his whereabouts, they went to him. The whole crowd was in distress or in debt. They were malcontents—about four hundred of them; but they gathered around David, who became their leader.

Now remember, David at this particular time was in exile, fleeing from King Saul for fear of his life. And what happened? Four hundred distressed people decided to follow him when he needed help himself.

We see something significant in this. There are in our society people with all kinds of needs. They are looking for leaders who can help them find solutions to their needs. They cannot solve their problems themselves. They have tried, but they get themselves in a bigger and bigger hole. Those four hundred people must have recognized that David had problems of his own. But he was the man who could not only get himself out of his mess, but also get them out of theirs. He had that quality of leadership. Lesson one: *Do not look for the flawless leader; look for the one with a heart for God.*

Lesson two comes from a reading of 1 Chronicles 11:

Then all Israel came together to David at Hebron, saying, "Indeed we are your bone and your flesh. Also, in time past, even when Saul was king, you were the one who led Israel out and brought them in; and the LORD your God said to you, 'You shall shepherd My people Israel, and be ruler over My people Israel.'" Therefore all the elders of Israel came to the king at Hebron, and David made a covenant with them at Hebron before the LORD. Then they anointed David king over Israel, according to the word of the LORD by Samuel (vv. 1-3).

The people in this story, by contrast, already had a sense of mission. They recognized that the well-being of the people of Israel necessitated good leadership and they identified David as the man to take charge. They came to him and said, "Listen, something needs to be done about Israel. You're the man to do it. Count on us; we identify with you."

There is no point in saying we need leadership if we are not prepared to identify personally with that leadership. Lesson two: *When you find a leader with a heart for God, commit yourself fully as a follower.*

If we turn to 1 Chronicles 12, we read of yet another lesson from David's life. Some Benjamites and other friends from Judah also approached David for guidance. David met them and said,

"If you have come peaceably to me to help me, my heart will be united with you; but if to betray me to my enemies, since there is no wrong in my hands, may the God of our fathers look and bring judgment." Then the Spirit came upon Amasai, chief of the captains, and he said:

"We are yours, O David;
We are on your side, O son of Jesse!
Peace, peace to you,
And peace to your helpers!
For your God helps you."

So David received them, and made them captains of the troop (vv. 17-18).

Lesson three: *The Holy Spirit will unite the leader with his followers.* People with a heart for God will know their shepherd. The godly leader will motivate people who want to be a part of what he is doing, and they will cooperate.

Are you that kind of leader? Do you recognize that kind of leadership or support it? You will if God has your heart.

ACCOUNTABILITY

I well remember as a boy in England, when we were about to graduate from high school, we used to have a particularly boring tradition called "Speech Day." We had to sit and listen to all kinds of monotonous speeches.

There was a certain man, a miner who lived in the area, who became involved in local politics. He had worked through the unions and had become one of the area leaders of the Socialist party. He was "elevated to the peerage" and changed his name from Jack Adams to Lord Adams and his wife became Lady Adams.

This event was highly amusing to everyone because he never got his "h's" right. He called himself "Lord Hadams" and his wife "Lady Hadams." The school authorities had Lord Adams speak at Speech Day. He got up and said, "Now, boys and girls, I want you to know hive done ha lot for your city hand this whole harea of Hengland. But I want you to hunderstand that hive been doing ha lot for Lord Hadams, too."

At least he was an honest man in that regard. What he was saying was, "I accepted the leadership to help feather my own nest."

Let's face it. Some leaders are on an ego trip. They love the economics of leadership. Some are power hungry. Thus, we have to remember to look for another quality of leadership—accountability.

Scripture teaches there is an ultimate accountability— the fear of God. We are to lead or to follow in the fear of God. Always remember that as shepherd or sheep you are finally accountable to the One who is the source of righteousness. It is in the fear of Him, in our accountability to

Him, that we are to exercise our role. And that is a very safe reminder for all of us.

LEADERSHIP AND UPLIFT

Note the tremendous expression that David used in 2 Samuel 23:4 in describing good leadership. He said godly rule is "like the light of the morning when the sun rises,/ A morning without clouds."

I love a sunrise. There is no time on earth like the dawn. It is beautiful, promising, and uplifting. It is amazing how people perk up at its radiance. David said the sun rising over the horizon is a picture of good leadership. This quality of leadership enables people to be uplifted, to be encouraged, and to be given a sense of hope. How our churches, families, and society as a whole need quality leadership that reflects dawn's sense of promise!

Not only that, David said true leadership is as refreshing as the rain. Recall your yard at the end of the summer. It has been particularly hot and dry, and the grass is brown. Then, toward the end of the summer, it rains, and overnight there is a different smell in the air. There is a new sparkle about the place, and the green grass comes through all over again.

Good leadership is like that. God sends His chosen leaders into the dry, brown, parched areas of life, and they bring a new glisten, a new sense of refreshment. That is what society needs and what our families demand, and frankly, that is what the church wants, too.

David was more than just a man for his time. In setting his heart to direct God's people, he was more than an example for us to follow. In truth, he was an instrument of leadership God actually used to model how the One who would occupy His throne would reign over us in the twentieth century.

A PERPETUAL KINGDOM

The reason this is true is because of what Isaiah wrote in his prophecy:

> For unto us a Child is born,
> Unto us a Son is given;
> And the government will be upon His shoulder.
> And His name will be called
> Wonderful, Counselor, Mighty God,·
> Everlasting Father, Prince of Peace.
> Of the increase of His government and peace
> There will be no end,
> Upon the throne of David and over His kingdom,
> To order it and establish it with judgment and justice
> From that time forward, even forever.
> The zeal of the LORD of hosts will perform this
> (Is. 9:6-7).

This prophetic statement deals with a Child who is to be born and a Son who is to be given. Notice the difference—the *born* Child and the *given* Son. Christ was born as a human Child from the womb of the Virgin Mary. But who is He? The eternal Son of God who is given as a precious gift for our salvation. As the One who is fully God and fully man, He will have the government, the authority, resting on His shoulders. He has the ability not only to carry His own load but also the load of all the people in the whole world who turn to Him. That is leadership.

Isaiah continued describing Him. He is the Wonderful Counselor, the Mighty God, the Father of Eternity, the Prince of Peace. His government will be endless; He will reign on David's throne. He will establish a Kingdom characterized by justice and righteousness, which will go on forever.

Do you see the clear link between David as leader and Messiah as Prince? Notice that Messiah will sit on David's throne and perpetuate it into eternity. In other words, the record of David's kingdom can in many instances serve as a picture of the eternal Kingdom that our Lord and Savior came to establish. David as a leader can be taken legitimately as an illustration of Christ as Lord.

1. The authority of Christ

The Lord Jesus made it abundantly clear that absolutely anybody could come to Him. Whosoever will, may come, is the gospel invitation. Jesus said in Matthew 11:28-29, "Come to Me, all you who labor and are heavy laden, and I will give you rest." He continued, "Take My yoke upon you and learn from Me." It isn't *just* an invitation. Whosoever will, may come, is part of it. The other part is, when you come to the Lord Jesus Christ, it is on the understanding that you render your allegiance to His authority. Then you will find rest for your soul.

Does that bring to mind any of the people from David's past? It sounds like those people who came to the cave of Adullam with their sense of need, does it not?

Many people come to Christ out of their great sense of need. They have made a travesty of their lives; they have tried to sort things out, but nothing works. They did not have time for Christ while things were going well. But now things are all amiss. They go to church and come to believe in the Lord Jesus as Savior. But not just as Savior. Because they come with a deep sense of need and distress, their solution brings more than eternal salvation somewhere off in the future. That would be good enough, mind you. But there is more. The Lord Jesus will meet their needs today as they give allegiance to Him. This is the authoritative aspect of the lordship of Christ. He deserves, He desires, He demands one's allegiance. He is Lord of all.

David welcomed to his cave all that motley crew of people on one condition: he was in charge. How else could they have operated together? What a picture of the church!

Our Lord Jesus opens wide His arms, and He says, "Whosoever will, may come, but on one condition—I'm in charge." Did you come to Him like that? Was your heart motivated toward God by a sense of need? In the desire for the meeting of your needs, have you come to recognize Christ's authority, His lordship?

Different people come different ways, but there must be one constant. He must become their leader. Whichever route you took to Christ—and there are many ways of getting to Him—when you get there, make sure of one thing, that He is Lord.

2. The absoluteness of Christ

The second aspect of Christ's lordship is that it is absolute. It is not open to negotiation. He is Lord over everything.

There is something about authority that rubs us the wrong way. Have you noticed? We do not like it.

I remember going to a ball game years ago and having the whole game spoiled for me by a guy sitting behind me complaining about his boss. "Nobody's gonna tell *me* what to do," he said. The philosophy is all too common. That is how many of us have operated in life. But then we come to Christ, and as soon as we are baptized and brought into the church, the pastor offers us some directive guidance from the Word of God. And we find ourselves bristling against this new authority.

If you had the feeling that everything was going to be great when you came to Christ and it isn't, I'll tell you why. You're having heart trouble. You may need some healing, some softening before the Lord because you have an ongoing rebellion deep in your heart against His lordship. That's why. I know, because there is something of that disease in all of us. And it is not much fun having a running battle with the Lord.

There is something else that is not very enjoyable either. The Lord has a habit of convicting us about our ongoing disobedience. If you give careful attention to the Word of God and you are living in disobedience, He will reprove you. If you are committed to the fellowship of believers in the church and you are rebellious to the authority—if they are doing their job—you will be disciplined and corrected. If the preacher is doing his job, uniting the people in the Holy Spirit, the Spirit of God will bring conformity to Christ. For the hard of heart, that is an uneasy feeling. There is an abrasiveness to the lordship of Christ for those who are rebellious and disobedient. It is something we need to face at the outset. Life in Christ is not always a picnic. And there is only one solution to it: Get back in line and let Him lead. He must be Lord.

3. The attraction to Christ

There is an attractive aspect to Christ's lordship. It is beautifully expressed for us in the words of David's final psalm. Listen:

> He who rules over men must be just,
> Ruling in the fear of God [as did our Lord Jesus].
> And he shall be like the light of the morning
>   when the sun rises,
> A morning without clouds,
> Like the tender grass springing out of the earth,
> By clear shining after rain (2 Sam. 23:3-4).

Do you know the Lord Jesus that way? Do you seek to live in obedience to Him? Is your overwhelming desire to acknowledge His authority and to give Him your full allegiance?

If that is your desire, I have a great promise for you. It is that you will know daily the radiant promise of new direction as He rises in your heart as fresh and radiant as the sunrise. You can anticipate the future and fruitful experience of a fresh purpose, as He irrigates the garden of your life with the freshness of the rain. He will bring the dry, barren dullness of unbelief to light. That is what He promised.

CHAPTER TWELVE

A Heart for God

"Now He said to me, 'It is your son Solomon who shall build My house and My courts; for I have chosen him to be My son, and I will be his Father. Moreover I will establish his kingdom forever, if he is steadfast to observe My commandments and My judgments, as it is this day.' Now therefore, in the sight of all Israel, the congregation of the LORD, and in the hearing of our God, be careful to seek out all the commandments of the LORD your God, that you may possess this good land, and leave it as an inheritance for your children after you forever...."

Then David gave his son Solomon the plans for the vestibule, its houses, its treasuries, its upper chambers, its inner chambers, and the place of the mercy seat; and the plans for all that he had by the Spirit, of the courts of the house of the LORD, of all the chambers all around, of the treasuries of the house of God, and of the treasuries for the dedicated things; also for the division of the priests and the Levites, for all the work of the service of the house of the LORD, and for all the articles of service in the house of the LORD....

And David said to his son Solomon, "Be strong and of good courage, and do it; do not fear nor be dismayed, for the LORD God—my God—will be with you. He will not leave you nor forsake you, until you have finished all the work for the service of the house of the LORD" (1 Chr. 28:6-8, 11-13,20).

A man approached me recently with a penetrating question. "Tell me something," he asked. "Why was David, with all the mistakes he made and the sins he got into, still so mightily used of God?"

I said, "If I were perfectly honest with you, I'd have to tell you that it's something of a mystery—given all the outright evil schemes he laid and the consequences of those acts. And yet, there's no question about it: the Scriptures, after carefully showing all these things, still portray him as a man forgiven, cleansed, and blessed—a man highly regarded by God." I paused to think for a moment, then continued. "Underlying everything that he did wrong and everything that happened, there was a deeper fundamental factor present in David's life. He had a heart for God."

Later, I thought again about that little expression, *a heart for God.* And the more I thought about it, the more convinced I became that this *is* the underlying theme of the life of David. He isn't shown as being perfect; he isn't described as a model of absolute righteousness. Instead, he is portrayed as an ordinary, strong-willed, impetuous person who made terrible mistakes and committed awful sins with dreadful consequences. But underlying it all, there was always that heart for God. He knew of God's mercy and was sincere in his repentance. In fact, he was known as a man after God's own heart (see 1 Sam. 13:14).

Having the Lord say such things about you never cancels out testing and even disappointment. Making peace with

God does not mean getting one's own way from then on. Adam, after all, never re-entered the garden of innocence. Moses was not allowed to lead Israel into the land of promise. And David, even with his heart for God, was not given permission to build the Temple.

But it was *because* his heart was righteous that he took that judgment as a man of God and obeyed the Lord.

A HOPE DEFERRED

David, of course, had reached old age. He cherished a great desire to build a temple for the Lord. But the Lord told him he would not be allowed to do it because he was a man of war. God had chosen David's son Solomon (the name *Solomon* is related to *shalom*, meaning "peace") to build the Temple.

Was David disappointed? Unquestionably he was. But how did he respond? He went about making meticulous preparations for the construction project. He knew Solomon was very young and inexperienced, so David set about to do the legwork for him. He procured materials, hired workmen, drew up the plans, and organized everything. You can just hear him mutter as he goes about his work: "And all the kid's got to do when it is time is put it up."

So David spent his last days absorbed with his project. Not only that, he also gathered the future leaders of the nation together and talked to them about running things after he was gone. And he sought to prepare Solomon, who would be king in his place. It was very obvious. His heart was burning for his God, and he was eager to see the spark ignite in the hearts of the leaders who would carry the torch after he was gone.

Many men, toward the end of a full life, settle for golf and a rocking chair, spending their potentially still fruitful years in less than eternally productive pursuits. They say, "I've done my part. Now let the younger ones take over."

Without in any way denying the validity of well-earned retirement or the necessity for older people to make way for younger leaders, I feel it is unfortunate when God's people do not grasp the opportunities that come their way in their older years. As a pastor, I have rejoiced recently to see key people in our congregation recognizing the value of well-aged wisdom. Many are investing their later years in a wide variety of ministries, ranging from overseas outreach to prison and hospital visitation to various types of eldership involvement in the church.

Let me urge you to decide in your heart today that you will maintain an active and aggressive walk with the Lord in your later years. It may be that your richest years of service to Christ and His church lie ahead of you! Remember, there is no such thing as being a retired overcomer.

You see, what we must make note of here is this: there is more to the Christian life than merely entering the race. The important thing about the race ultimately is how we finish it. The reality of our ongoing spiritual life is that having maintained throughout life a heart for God, at the end of our days our heart for God is still there. Having served God all our lives, we must never slump into an attitude of demanding our rights at the end.

For King David, having a heart for God dramatically governed several areas of his life. It meant that he had a heart for God's glory, a heart for God's work—to serve Him until the end of his days—and a heart for God's people.

A HEART FOR GOD'S GLORY

When the children of Israel were in the desert, God had told Moses that they must have a tabernacle or a tent as the center of their worship and their encampment. In that tabernacle, that dwellingplace of God, was to be placed the Ark of the Covenant. Whenever they moved, it was always to have preferential treatment on the journey. And when they were stationary, it was always in the center of their camp. So the Ark of the Covenant and the tent of meeting, as they called it, were predominant in their spiritual life.

By David's time, of course, Israel was no longer a nomadic tribe. They were settled into urban centers. Jerusalem had become the capital city of the people of Israel. So David reasoned that if a tent was right for the desert, a house of cedar was right for the Lord's dwellingplace in Jerusalem.

Why did David feel so strongly the necessity to have that temple built? Because he was concerned that God's glory should be expressed in the very center of the society over which he had reigned. But before that temple—that expression of God's glory—was going to become a reality, he had to be able to explain to the people his vision for God's glory, which was still burning in his heart.

Remember, God made an everlasting covenant with His people. He had committed Himself to them. As the Scriptures teach, He became their God; they became His people. And for David, the covenant was part of the glory of God.

Can you imagine it? God, who made the heavens and the earth and inhabits eternity, is interested enough in people like us to reach out and promise us He will be our God forever, and invite and encourage us to be His people. He is not remote or removed, out of touch, or aloof. In fact, He wants our love, and He wants us to know how much He loves us. That is the glory of God.

So King David was saying, "We need a visible expression of that glory, down here in the middle of Jerusalem." Although he was an old man, he set out to make sure his vision for the Temple became a reality.

You will remember that above the Ark of the Covenant was a cover on which the two cherubim were facing each other. The ark was regarded as the earthly throne of God. It was seen as that place where the God who sits high in the heavens on His throne had a footstool down on earth; the ark was sometimes called "the footstool." It was the place where the heights of the throne of God touched the earth.

This is another important picture for us to see and understand about the Lord. He is high and holy and separate from sin. But even though He is enthroned in glory, He reaches down to earth; as heaven is His throne, so earth is His footstool. If we are to have an experience of Him, we must come, as it were, to His footstool. We must prostrate ourselves before Him in glad worship, and we must glorify Him.

David's experience of God's lovingkindness and tender mercies had been so rich, and his recognition of God's glory so profound, that he felt the tabernacle was no longer a suitable reflection of such a glorious God. It represented the transience of the wilderness journey; David wanted God's dwellingplace to be a permanent reminder of His glory in the midst of the promised land.

Apparently nobody else in Jerusalem was too concerned about it—perhaps they were too absorbed in beautifying their own homes and they had not noticed the tabernacle was incongruous in an urban setting. Unlike David, they apparently did not see that the glories of their own homes reflected very poorly when contrasted with the simple, folding structure of the Lord's dwellingplace. Perhaps they failed to recognize that their actions were a stark commentary on their spiritual priorities—or lack of them.

David's heart for God would not accept such a situation, and he took steps to rectify it. It was clear to David—a temple must be built, a temple that in some way would glorify God among a people prone to forgetting Him.

A HEART FOR GOD'S NAME

The house was also for "the name of the Lord." In Israel, the very name of God was regarded as being holy—so holy, in fact, the people would never repeat it themselves or write it in full. In some branches of Judaism today, they still will not write the name of God in full.

The "name of God" is, of course, an expression of His character. Thus when we look at the different names and titles of God, we study them with a view to understanding something of God's character or divine attributes. When David said, "We need a house for His name," he had in mind a house that would speak of all the different attributes of His nature. The Temple must be built!

It should not be too hard for us to understand David's concern. Many of our cities have memorials bearing inscriptions such as: *In Memory of our Heroic Dead.* Rome has her triumphal arches glorifying the exploits of her victorious emperors. The British Museum proudly displays the carvings from bygone monarchies, recording the glorious past. And whatever we may think of the cathedrals of Europe, there is no doubt that many of their soaring spires and vaulted roofs have contributed to lifting people's spirits to more glorious thoughts than those that reflected their non-Christian eras.

David was not interested in an empty memorial—he wanted a "working temple," a place not only alive with people actively worshiping and serving God, but also a place where the presence of the living God would be recognized and revered.

A HEART FOR GOD'S WORK

David, coming to the end of his days, was very concerned about who would take the baton from him, who would run the race after him. He wanted to ensure that those leaders had a heart for God's work. So he began to outline procedures, particularly to young Solomon. How delightful it is to hear old David giving out these instructions!

David's relations with his family, of course, were mixed.

No man ever had more traumatic experiences with his children. Some had been treacherous traitors, others ill-disciplined and licentious. Some had died awful deaths, others had performed dastardly acts. Solomon, born with a silver spoon in his mouth, was at this stage showing signs of being a man after his father's heart.

David, however, was taking no chances. He had learned early how easily the privileged can go sour, how slippery is the shape of those who live in high places. Solomon had too many things in his favor. It would require unusual self-discipline and devotion to maintain the vision of his father and to secure for himself a heart for God. Indifference to the Lord would be difficult to avoid.

Having a heart for God's work means that we live our lives in wholehearted submission to the Lord and His Word. We can find so many things that we need to do, so many demands on our time and our resources. The easiest thing in the world is to channel time, energy, and resources into 1001 legitimate things, but leave the work of the Lord for number 1002. The only thing I know that will get God's work into top priority is if we have established genuine submission of our hearts to Him. Because He is our Lord and our God, everything else must fit around Him.

Sometimes I fear that our Lord and God is not at the hub of our lives but is rather an appendage; He is a convenience item, a celestial "Mr. Fixit" to whom we turn for occasional help. A heart for God and a heart for God's work presuppose a tremendous sense of personal devotion and singlemindedness.

Such a heart requires a willingness to find areas of involvement designed by God for us as a means of expressing living appreciation to Him. It involves a commitment to that work of the church which tangibly expresses the commitment we profess to the Lord. And it also means a special reordering of our lives to that spiritual service which takes precedence over our many social activities—

thereby giving conclusive credibility to our claim that the Lord is indeed our God.

David reminded Solomon of something very important. It is not just *what* you do that matters; it is *why* and *how* you do it. God is going to be searching the heart, understanding the motives behind our thoughts and actions. If we have a heart for God and if it is channeled into His work, then from that heart will spring a desire for wholehearted service, not simply doing enough to get by or to look good to others.

The great need among God's people has always been that they would have a heart to work for Him whether anyone else is watching or not. We need a heart that plunges into God's work and forgets to check the church and society page in the paper the following day.

There is a place for appreciation and public affirmation of work for the Lord done well. A ministry of encouragement is certainly one of the most precious ministries of all. But if we become dependent upon affirmation and enamored with encouragement by others, there is a danger that we will become confused in our motives.

There are some servants of God who get bent out of shape if they are not recognized, others who quit if they feel they are not high enough in the pecking order to receive public accolades. The only safe motivation for us is one that recognizes that the Lord searches out our hearts while our brothers and sisters are more likely to observe our actions and only guess at our intentions. Don't be preoccupied with impressing people around you. Do what you do for the glory of God.

A heart to serve the Lord is a heart that seeks after the Lord *continually*. "Seek Him," said David to Solomon. "If you seek Him, He will be found by you; but if you forsake Him, He will cast you off forever" (1 Chr. 28:9).

Knowing God is like mining for silver. If you go after silver, you are going to have to do some digging. And it means you are *not* going to be doing a lot of other things that you would be doing in the time it takes to dig. And you will have to learn to be patient, because you will find far more debris than silver. You have to sift through everything you unearth to find the little chunks of silver. In the end, you may be surprised to realize how much more silver must be left to discover.

Knowing God is not a once and for all expedition. If you are to know God, you must continually seek after Him. It will take time and work. It takes a lifetime to really know Him. And remember, don't use shortcuts to know the Lord—they take too long! People who are casual and superficial want a God they will trip over while they are doing something else. They don't want a God they must seek.

You say, "Where do I start looking?"

In His Word.

"I can't understand it."

That is the attitude of somebody who wants silver, but doesn't want mining. A person who seeks after God knows there is no greater thing in life than to truly know Him.

How is it that David at the end of his days, in passing the baton to his son Solomon, could say, "Be strong and of good courage, and do it; do not fear nor be dismayed, for the LORD God—my God—will be with you. He will not leave you nor forsake you, until you have finished all the work for the service of the house of the LORD" (1 Chr. 28:20)? It is precisely because *this was the whole story of David's life.* God had been faithful to David. Through all the dilemmas of his life—the times of rebellion, rejection, and repentance—the elder statesman of Israel knew one thing! God had stayed with him.

Can you make a similar statement?

I want to encourage you that if you will but set your heart on the things of God each and every day for the remainder of your life, His faithfulness to you will be overwhelming. Are there sins in your life? Drop them! Have you twisted the will of God? Repent of it, now. Move back today to the center of the track. Do you worry about the future? Give your future to Christ. Tomorrow and what it may bring are not your business or your burden.

The world—and the church—so desperately needs people at this very hour who are committed to a life of godliness and singleness of purpose. Will you give the Lord your heart—all of it? For good? Tell Him so as you close the cover on these pages. And set about for the rest of your days to be obedient to every facet of His will.

Settle for nothing less than *a heart for God*.

Enhancing Teaching and Learning

2nd Edition, Revised

**A Leadership Guide for School
Library Media Specialists**

Jean Donham

Neal-Schuman Publishers, Inc.
New York   London

Published by Neal-Schuman Publishers, Inc.
100 William St., Suite 2004
New York, NY 10038

Printed and bound in the United States of America.

The paper used in this publication meets the minimum requirements of American National Standard for Information Sciences—Permanence of Paper for Printed Library Materials, ANSI Z39.48-1992.

Library of Congress Cataloging-in-Publication Data

Donham, Jean.
    Enhancing teaching and learning : a leadership guide for school library media specialists / Jean Donham.—2nd ed., rev.
        p. cm.
    Includes bibliographical references and indexes.
    ISBN 978-1-55570-647-0 (alk. paper)
    1. School libraries—United States. 2. Instructional materials centers—United States. I. Title.

Z675.S3D65 2008
027.8′0973—dc22
                                                        2008023321